PHANTOM LIMBS

PETER SZENDY

ON MUSICAL BODIES

PHANTOM LIMBS

Translated by Will Bishop

FORDHAM UNIVERSITY PRESS)) NEW YORK)) 2016

This work was originally published in French as Peter Szendy, *Membres fantômes. Des corps musiciens* © 2002 Les Editions de Minuit.

Ouvrage publié avec le concours du Ministère français chargé de la Culture–Centre National du Livre.

This work has been published with the assistance of the French Ministry of Culture–National Center for the Book.

Fordham University Press also publishes its books in a variety of electronic formats. Some content that appears in print may not be available in electronic books.

Visit us online at www.fordhampress.com.

Library of Congress Cataloging-in-Publication Data

Szendy, Peter.
[Membres fantômes des corps musiciens. English]
Phantom limbs : on musical bodies / Peter Szendy ; translated by Will Bishop.
pages cm
Includes bibliographical references.
ISBN 978-0-8232-6705-7 (cloth : alk. paper) — ISBN 978-0-8232-6706-4 (pbk. : alk. paper)
1. Music—Philosophy and aesthetics. 2. Human body in music. I. Bishop, Will, translator. II. Title.
ML3800.S96813 2016
781.1—dc23

2015023328

Printed in the United States of America

18 17 16 5 4 3 2 1

First edition

FOR JEAN-LUC NANCY

At first some gibberish about vibrating
strings and sensitive fibers . . .

—Denis Diderot, *D'Alembert's Dream*

CONTENTS

PHANTOM LIMBS

Training

I am here in this cool room on the ground floor, in a house that exists today only in my memories (it burned down).

Its main occupant is the piano. On the piano, a plaster cast: Beethoven. It's incredibly kitsch, especially when it's lit up. But it is one element of the staging G. had set into place in his room, like the little sign he'd hung over the bed: "Nobody's perfect."

The white keys have yellowed and appear burnished. An innumerable number of fingers must have worn them out.

G. is teaching me to play a prelude whose name and author I don't yet know—and won't for quite a while. Nor will I know the notes, actually (I don't even know that something like notes exists).

Learning means: watching where he puts his fingers, memorizing the keys he presses down as you would identify the footprints of an animal you're tracking. With my gaze set on the keyboard at whose level I almost am (I emerge just barely above its height), I am under the impression that I will have to pour my body into the mobile, moving mold formed by the keys that G. pushes down or releases. Plastically, I will have to espouse this contour whose hollowed-out shape he has left for me. With the most intense attention, I register the deformations of the line of the keys, raised up in some places and drawn back in others. A crenulated, angled line. I will model my body on the empty envelope his body, fleetingly, leaves.

Behind the repetitive idiotism of my training (I spend days and weeks at it, and I must constantly ask him to show me once again the digital traces of his knowledge in order to fix them in my memory and reproduce them with my own fingers), there will have been this gripping experience: espousing another body. (When I recall these moments, I no longer know how many fingers, hands, and phalanges I have.)

But that's not all. There is also the piano's belly: its hollow, disemboweled, or eviscerated belly, its old emptied-out, upright Steinway interior, which had been equipped with a roller mechanism to allow it to play all by itself. G. had had this mechanism, which I imagine produced old, bad hits, taken out; he had had it removed, he said, to get a purer sonority. But there is still the little sliding door at eye level when I'm sitting on the stool; there is still this opening that attracts me to the secrets of its machinery. I can stick my little head into it, and in the darkness I can make out the hammers, levers, and felts. Resting in silence.

I can also play while I plunge into this vibrating piece of furniture. And it is when I do so that, with my ear up against the wires and in an acrobatic position, I absolutely forget my body, giving myself up body and soul to this improbable sound coupling or montage by which I reinvent myself even more formidably than in childhood games.

Today, this memory is indissociable from a dream that, timidly and in a low voice, accompanies it. If I had learned to play, not only by following in the tracks of his fingers but also by conforming to envelopes that were even ghostlier, by bending myself to the mechanical crenulations of the keys under the impetus of the turning roller, what bodies would I have espoused?

I now know that great musicians engraved their playing onto rolls and cylinders. This even has quite a history, much older than is often thought. Long before the recordings realized by Debussy on Welte-Mignon cylinders in 1912–13, there will have been, in 1775, a certain Father Engramelle, who, by inventing "tonotechnics" (that is to say, "the art of noting cylinders, and everything susceptible of being noted in the instruments of mechanical concerts"), was already having something like my dream: "We would still today enjoy the interpretations of Lully, Machand, and of all the great men who ravished their contemporaries with admiration . . . : Their best pieces they transmitted to posterity on several inalterable cylinders would have been conserved in this style of expression that we no longer have any idea of except through history."

Would I have been all these bodies—Lully, Couperin, Bach, Debussy, and even this Beethoven who looks at me all lit up? Would I have been their cohort, their theory? Would I have had their hands, their fingers? Would I have breathed with them? Would they have *possessed* me?

CHAPTER 1 **Interpreting Bodies**

I have a body: This is a statement that—even though its use and overuse have made it banal—vacillates and trembles in me every time I experience musical body-to-body contact [*corps à corps*].

Each time this phrase comes back to me, in a halo still rumbling around the resonating instrument, I sit there wondering what the verb *to have* might mean here. What does *having* a body, and a body that is *mine*, really mean when I lift my hands from the keyboard, and, in this suspended time, little by little, the vibrations, tacts, and contacts dissipate, and the innervations slowly come undone, the ones that just a moment ago seemed to articulate some kind of immense *demultiplication* table to me?

It sometimes seems to me that after the incredible dilation and ramification that my body has just experienced in its contact with keys, vibrating strings that resound or zing, pieces of wood and felts that strike in a muffled way or with brilliance, it retracts or reconfigures only reluctantly [*à contre-coeur*]. It is thus *despite my body* [*à contre-corps*]; yes, it is in a slow contraction that an infinite number of *phantom limbs* that had come to dance a delicious Sabbath wither away.

A transitory necrosis of an always unique form of my organism's organization.

And I tell myself that what was invented and disposed, provisionally and as if it were pending during the time devoted to playing, is a momentary figure, a fragile and fleeting envelope for what Nietzsche, through the voice of Zarathustra, called "the commander"—a "self" from before the "ego":

> Always the self listens and seeks; it compares, compels, conquers, destroys. It rules and is also the ruler of the ego.
>
> Behind your thoughts and feelings . . . stands a powerful commander, an unknown wise man—he is called self. He lives in your body, he is your body.[1]

Something—something unknown, an *x*—thus seems to inhabit my body; it seems to inhabit my body that I inhabit as well. And thanks to the grace of musical playing, it seems to move from behind to up front. It seems to *become embodied*—an almost tangible though infinitely plastic body—it seems to dance its dance for a while before retreating and leaving me dumbfounded, dispossessed.

What musician has not dreamed of virtuosity as a magisterial stage where the domination, possession, or mastery of this dancing chimera, this "self" that has furtively emerged from its threatening reserve, could play itself out, victoriously?

Because perhaps even more than a struggle with the instrument's inert matter, musical virtuosity might have something to do with the hand-to-hand combat [*corps à corps*] between an "ego" and a "self," in a kind of conjuration: It would be a ritual celebration—a magnificent one by its very despair—of a Promethean denial opposed to the commander of the ego, in the spectacle made of the mastery of playing. Liszt has stated it better than anyone, this dream of a tamer who is dialoguing with the unknown *x* to domesticate it; and this is the point where the piano became for him a docile *means of transport* to colonize the *terra incognita* and its uncanniness:

> My piano is to me what a ship is to the sailor, what a steed is to the Arab, and perhaps more because even now *my piano is myself*, my speech, and my life. It is the intimate personal depository of everything that stirred wildly in my brain during the most impassioned days of my youth. It was there that all my wishes, all my dreams, all my joys, and all my sorrows lay. Its strings quivered under all my passions, *its docile keys* obeyed my every whim.[2]

Here virtuosity is nothing other than a theater of domestication: After struggle and conquest, it installs the ego once again in its mastery. The virtuoso's body does not emerge from this recomposed but is merely glorified. It is he (the "I") that leaves a victorious seal on the matter that he informs or inspires, in order to erase all trace of a self crouching there, behind. (This is at least what Liszt says allows us to understand—which does not necessarily include the experience of hearing him play.)

Other forms of less dramatically conquering bodily struggle [*corps à corps*] seem to give voice to the instrument without immediately enlisting it into the project of its mastery.

In chamber music it readily presents the face of a dialogue. It's in a tone of familiar conversation that many teaching manuals destined for the use of amateurs address the instrument *in person* in the figure of a convivial prosopopoeia. In the second part of his marvelous 1676 *Musick's Monument*,[3] Thomas Mace, hoping to give us "the Lute made Easie," inserts "a Dialogue between the Author and his Lute." He asks his instrument, "What makes Thee sit so sad, my Noble Friend?"

And the instrument answers by complaining about the negligence and poor handling to which he has fallen victim from those who do not make the effort to learn to play it with respect.

But in this fiction of alterity, this domestic dialogue, the self that Zarathustra mentioned is conspicuous by its absence. The Lute presents itself as a partner, as a quiet roommate with whom one can do business and negotiate and that one will learn to play on good terms at the end of the conversation. Nothing about it suggests an unknown, worrisome *x*. It is, therefore, certainly not this reassuring accord concluded in the intimacy of a home that will be able to account for my strange experience (that I nonetheless know is shared and sharable): the radical reinvention or recomposition of the body, its renewed destitution and individuation, endowed with an unprecedented envelope and members.

Breaking with Lisztian metonymy ("my piano is myself," it's my part for the whole), breaking as well with the prosopopoeia of the speaking lute, there is one figure—that I do not know how to name—through which Thomas Bernhard, in his fiction inspired by the character of Glenn Gould, will have approached the fragile reality, the *suspended* reality of these chimeras of the body whose tangible plasticity and infinite becoming are confirmed for me every time I have an experience of the piano.

In *The Loser*, Gould declares:

> My ideal would be, *I would be the Steinway, I wouldn't need Glenn Gould.* . . . I could, by being the Steinway, make Glenn Gould totally superfluous. But not a single piano player has ever managed to make himself superfluous by being Steinway, as Glenn said. To wake up one day *and be Steinway and Glenn in one, . . . Glenn Steinway, Steinway Glenn.*[4]

This fantastic and fantastical reciprocal baptism inscribes Glenn Steinway at the heart of an entire onomastic lineage of composite names that cross over all the borders between different musical genres: Banjo Joe, Johnny Guitar Watson, *The Man with the Horn*. But the chimera named Glenn Steinway is different from the others to the precise extent that the incarnation and living incorporation of this bifid name is pushed back onto an ideal, unattainable horizon. Whereas Johnny Guitar or Banjo Joe still seem to be sustained by a possible conviviality with the instrument (which is not without recalling Mace's dialogue),[5] Glenn Steinway infinitely defers his becoming embodied by enduring the following paradox: There will be Glenn Steinway only once Glenn, having become "superfluous," will have definitively dissolved into a Steinway *playing all by itself*.

This dream of an organic body deposed and transfigured by its replacement in an instrumental automatism, this "ideal," as Gould says in the novel, nonetheless also seems to me to fail to grasp the singularity of the experience for which I'd like to account by showing its historical importance: that of an invention, of a *manufacture* of the body, which would certainly not be the work of an ego consciously or conscientiously cultivating its capacities of execution, but which would also not be included in the horizon of a sacrifice at the altar of inorganic objectivity. This is then a manufacture or a fiction (in the sense of something made, *fictum-factum*), in which the self would seek to open the path for unprecedented organs, making use of a musical hand-to-hand struggle that must above all not be reduced to one of its terms: neither triumphant and virtuosic Glenn nor Steinway alone, but the chance for the tension and reciprocal innervation of both, one that the chimerical figure of Glenn-Steinway seems able to name only with reluctance, despite his body [*à son corps défendant*].

In its relation to an ideal horizon, Gould's dream does indeed have something *sacrificial* about it: The ego (Glenn) will deliver himself up body and soul to the *autophonia* of the instrument vibrating by itself. Yet by sacrificing himself in this way, by making himself superfluous, it is perhaps still Glenn who, in the novel, dreams of finding a way to get along just fine, that is, without owing anything else to the self.

Is what is intolerable in all this—which all the virtuosic conquests, all the reassuring dialogues, and all the sacrifices attempt to conjure up as a way of getting rid of it—not that incredibly insistent adverb in Zarathustra's statement: "*Always* the self listens and seeks"?

If so, how might we understand the insistence or authority of this self that seems to find in the musical body-to-body contact [*corps à corps*] the occasion, the chance for which it is on the lookout? How might we describe the clearing work that the self, this path-breaker, performs in the body's envelope?

Nietzsche played piano; we have testimony to this from several people. "I do not believe," writes his friend Carl Gersdorff, "Beethoven's improvisations could have been more poignant than those of Nietzsche, especially when a storm filled the sky."[6] And Peter Gast, who pays him a visit toward the end of his life, after his hospitalization, recounts: "Nothing but phrases of a Tristan-like inspiration, *pianissimo*; then fanfares of trombones and trumpets, a Beethoven-like furor, exultant songs, meditations, reveries—indescribable!"[7]

One should not rush to see Nietzsche's musical body-to-body experiences [*corps à corps*] as the symptoms of an unconscious that might become manifest through the vehicle of music and even more clearly in the period said to be of his "madness." The self that, through these several descriptions, one can make out playing behind the ego, and probably even in front of him, this self is not the unconscious of psychoanalysis, even if it is tempting to make Nietzsche into its precursor. This is why, if it is obviously impossible to maintain that it is "I" who is speaking here at the piano, one probably also and still has to give up on the desire to decipher the inscription of a body subject to drives, of an "it speaks." "Perhaps," writes Nietzsche, "some day we shall accustom ourselves . . . to get along without the little 'it' (which is all that is left of the honest little old ego)."[8]

What seems to emerge in musical playing, what seems to find its chance or its grasp in an exemplary way, might well be *interpretation*, on the condition that we understand this word not in its usual musical sense, but in the sense Nietzsche could give it in a fragment from 1885–86: "When an organ is constructed," he says, "it is a question of interpretation"; or elsewhere: "The organic process constantly presupposes a continual interpretation."[9]

Musical interpretation, playing, taken in a Nietzschean sense rather than in its usual musical sense, would perhaps be this organic thrust not only removed from the ego's command but also unlinked from the drive of an id that would remain related to it in an underground way. Thus the musical body-to-body experience would produce inventions of improbable bodies that are still without figure or destination. Bodies that are neither monstrous nor fabulous, neither glorious nor weak nor empty: simple but powerful thrusts from even before the drives, from "behind"; threads or traces of still unorganized organs—neither living nor dead—that are membering, dismembering, hurrying, crowding, growing, ramifying.

CHAPTER 2 Effictions

The postures of Nietzsche's body at the piano apparently had nothing to envy the veritable *trance of possession* Diderot staged in *Rameau's Nephew*:

> But you would have gone off into roars of laughter at the way he mimicked the various instruments. With cheeks puffed out and a hoarse, dark tone he did the horns and bassoons, a bright, nasal tone for the oboes, quickening his voice with incredible agility for the stringed instruments to which he tried to get the closest approximation; he whistled the recorders and cooed the flutes, shouting, singing, and throwing himself about like a mad thing: a one-man show . . . , a whole orchestra . . . tearing up and down, stopping, like one possessed, with flashing eyes and foaming mouth.[1]

Possessed, yes, the Nephew most certainly is that; and this is why he, too, does not *have* his body.

What is incredible is that this possession is not the result of one or several minds, as one might think if one limits oneself to the most theatrical passages of his trance (when he "plays" roles or "mimics" characters, men and women, singers and dancers). No, the Nephew has a body that he does not have to the precise extent that he *begins* by letting himself be possessed by other *bodies*, sound-producing and vibrating bodies that interpret him as much as he interprets them.

It is true, though, that during some of these transports, he also lends his voice to living beings and lively passions: "What didn't he do? He wept, laughed, sighed, his gaze was tender, soft, or furious: a woman swooning with grief, a poor wretch abandoned in the depth of his despair." But the privilege of welcoming other souls into one's body is an absolutely provisional one; it is abolished once the murmurings of the sounds of nature take things up: when the Nephew becomes "waters murmuring in a cool, solitary place or tumbling in torrents down the mountain side," and then "a thunderstorm, a hurricane," and also the "howling of the tempest" and "the crash of thunder."

Possessed *by nature*, the Nephew then gets lost in the night; even in his very muteness he is delivered up body and soul to the unknown, to the *x*:

> [He was] night with its shadows, darkness and silence, for even silence itself can be depicted in sound. By now he was quite beside himself. Knocked up with fatigue, like a man coming out of a deep sleep or long trance, he stood there motionless, dazed, astonished.

Astonishing Nephew who can even mime silence.

Or rather: who seems able to be silent, as in and of himself, only by *being silence itself*, possessed by a figure without figure.

And this is why one could not say when, exactly, he emerges from the trance. One could not say if his fatigue and stupor are already on the side of the return of "*his* strength and memory" (as Diderot writes, apparently placing his trust in a possessive that he has nonetheless dispossessed), or if they still belong to his crazy pantomime painting even silence.

The consequences of a mimetic possession of the body *by silence itself* could be immense, incalculable. What would remain of a body said to be "one's own" if its muteness, its silence, and immobile being-there, is still a *figure*, even a *haunting*?

It is true that the Nephew's body is a fictional body (*fictum*). It is a fabricated body, in two different ways: It has its place only in pages that recount and shape it; and, in these pages, it borrows its consistency, perhaps even its mere stance or making, from other bodies of which it is composed, of which it is made (*factum*).

The Nephew owes all his appearance to the *effiction* Diderot gives of it, in the sense of that old figure of rhetoric (*effictio*) that designated the verbal description of a body, in general from head to toe.[2]

I cannot, however, stop myself from lending an ear to other meanings in the name of this outdated figure: I also understand *effiction* as the contraction into one word of fiction and its power, of its *efficacy*. A new-old figure, then, that would state *fiction in effect(s)*.

Now the chance inscribed into this word opens the possibility of describing and naming, quite precisely, the consistency, or the strange modality of insistence and persistence, the peculiar *agency* of phantom limbs and organs that the musical body-to-body experience causes to emerge.

Because manifestly, they don't take place in the sense that a weighing and individuated body occupies (some) space. Their taking-place would rather be related to that of fictive bodies, like the Nephew's. And yet they are not mere semblances of bodies, like those that the disincarnated world of sounds promises us.[3] These bodies have a consistency, a persistence, or a *way of remaining* [*restance*] that I experience;

and above all, beyond what I experience of it, they are deposited and survive in sequences of active fictions, in a *chain of effictions.*

It is indeed in this way, through effictive sequences, that music makes, or fictions, organs, hands, fingers, palms, phalanges, feet, backs, cavities, skins, membranes, pads—and therefore also prehensions and tacts that, even if they cannot be assigned to attested and known bodies (for example, human bodies), are nonetheless *in the process of becoming embodied.*

With a bit of patience, I hope I'll be able to exhibit *tangible* traces of these bodies that, without being down here among biologically noted organisms, are not *out there* either, in a fictive or fabulous ("mysterical")[4] elsewhere. Let us say—for this is what we will have to say and demonstrate over and over again—that they are *there*, but with a being-there that, as we will see, is certainly not without its effects, once all is said and done, on the very idea of the *there.*

Before getting to the long sequence of effictions awaiting us, and as a way of giving in advance the principle of their sequencing, I would like to linger a while longer with Diderot, a great thinker of bodies and organs and a surprising *organologist.*

If we follow certain of his other fictions, it may well turn out to be that the "I" at the keyboard allows itself to be possessed, so to speak, or *interpreted*, by words that have come from far away, that were on the lookout for this chance to take (as one says with an intransitive turn of phrase that a graft *takes*). My body-to-body experience [*corps à corps*] with the keyboard would then become the moment that *representations of bodies*, up until then only pending, were waiting in order to *precipitate.* And one would be entitled to say, using a Nietzschean vocabulary, that the "self" looking out for this occasion has the consistency of a weave of words.[5]

Sitting at my keyboard, I have, for example, often thought of Diderot's reply that, in his *Conversation* with d'Alembert, gave voice to the fiction of a keyboard-body. He assuredly made of it an effective, that is to say effictive, fiction. Here, he declared, is what led him "to compare the fibers that make up our sense organs with sensitive, vibrating strings":

> A sensitive, vibrating string goes on vibrating and sounding long after it has been plucked. . . . But vibrating strings have yet another property, that of making others vibrate, and it is in this way that one idea calls up a second, and the two together a third, and all three a fourth, and so on; you can't set a limit to the ideas called up and linked together by a philosopher meditating or communing with himself in silence and darkness. This instrument [i.e., "the philosopher-instrument"] can make astonishing leaps, and one idea called up will sometimes start an harmonic at an incomprehensible interval. If this phenomenon can be observed between resonant strings which are inert and separate, why should it not take place between living and connected points, continuous and sensitive fibers? . . . And in my opinion this is all that happens in a clavichord organized like you and me.[6]

This reply will have made more than a few people dream. The first to have done so is d'Alembert, who, in the famous *Dream* that interrupts the *Conversation*, relives in a dream and in his agitated body the efficacy of fiction. He is as if transfixed, as I myself regularly am, by the effiction of a body-instrument made tangible. Diderot's words will have literally *possessed* d'Alembert in his sleeping and agitated body. A beginning, a first possible seismic impact in a long sequence of effictions that spread from one body to another.

The contagion actually begins in this surprising performative first addressed to d'Alembert in the *Conversation* before the *Dream*: "But *you will dream*," Diderot predicts for him.

"You will dream about this talk when your head is on your pillow, and if it doesn't *gain consistency*, it will be too bad" (my emphasis, of course).

You *will be*, he says in sum, a clavichord-body. For a while—for the long while of words.

These words that *take*, these words that end up consisting through their insistence, would thus sculpt an embodying [*faire-corps*] that is diffused through resonances. D'Alembert will have been the first to have been gripped by the dream Diderot whispered to him. But very quickly this dream attains other bodies. Thus does the Doctor Bordeu, called by Mademoiselle de l'Espinasse to the sickbed of poor d'Alembert to watch over this first dreamer, also begin to vibrate in unison with the effictive words. To Mademoiselle de l'Espinasse, who asks him, "Are you dreaming, too?" Bordeu answers, "I would almost undertake to tell you what comes next" (169), that is to say what comes after in d'Alembert's dream, which is thus propagated from body to body, from voice to voice.

One will speak for the other, will give his voice to the other, possessed by fictions dictated to and by the other. This is how words are passed that sculpt transfixed bodies. And Mademoiselle de l'Espinasse can thus declare: "I can now proclaim to all the world that there is no difference between a doctor awake and a philosopher dreaming" (170).

Diderot-d'Alembert-Bordeu are a sequence. Even better: They resonate within each other, and the dream spreads.

With one voice diffracted into their bodies, they (he) speak(s) of "a certain tension," of a "tone," of "a normal energy which governs the real or imaginary extent of the body." And if they (he) say(s) it is "real or imaginary," that's because "as the tension, tone, or energy are variable, our bodies are not always of the same volume" (197).

There is no doubt no chance in the fact that they (he) name(s) here "tone," the *tonos* which was indeed for the

Greeks the *tension* of the instruments with sensitive strings that we are.[7] Instruments that, as Bordeu prettily puts it when speaking of memory and imagination, "re-cord" one another [*se recordent*].

But, however strung and re-corded [*cordés et recordés*] they may be in the propagated memory of ancient or recent fictions, sonorous bodies are constantly weaving new ones, which are waiting, pending, to *consist* effictively.

Some of the exchanges between Bordeu and Mademoiselle de l'Espinasse thus suggest an open list that will have preceded all fiction. In them, it's a question of "threads," that is to say of the strings or innervations that give birth to our sensory organs; and the two interlocutors explicitly envisage the possibility that, beyond the five (or six) counted ones, others are *in waiting*:

> *Bordeu:* The rest of the threads go to form as many other varieties of touch as there are differences between the organs and parts of the body. *Mademoiselle de l'Espinasse:* What are they called? I have never heard of them. *Bordeu:* They have no names. (187–88)

If it is true, as I will patiently attempt to show, that music brings about numerous proliferations of these organs and their tacts, these members and membranes, who will name them? Who will record them in their infinite nomenclature? Who will *pass them on* and in what sequences of effictive fictions? Who will inscribe them and on what surfaces, in what media?

CHAPTER 3 Organologics (1): The Erasure of Bodies

Organology (from the Greek *organon*, which means the instrument as well as the body) should be the first of the fictions for us to follow since it presents itself as a science, in other words, the descriptive study, classification, and nomenclature of bodies that produce sound and music.

But besides the fact that organology is a relatively recent corpus of discourse in the West, its fictional efficacy first consisted in *evacuating the body*. For the authors of treatises on music, for quite a long time music quite simply had no body. We will have to be patient to make our way through organology to gain access to what it nonetheless ended up recording of the multiple becoming of sonorous bodies. We will also need a few acts of force—and a few asides.

"A musician [*musicus*] is someone who possesses the capacity to judge according to speculation and reason."

It is no doubt with this phrase from Boethius and a few others in the same vein that the history of Western music begins. Against the background of a tripartite division that distinguished between *musica mundana*, *musica humana*, and the music of instruments,[1] *musicus* has been defined, since Boethius and for a long time after him, in opposition with two other types. Nasty types, actually:

> Thus, there are three classes [*genera*] of those who are engaged in the musical art. The first class consists of those who perform on instruments [*instrumentis agitur*], the second of those who compose songs [*fingit carmina*], and the third of those who judge instrumental performance and song [*instrumentorum opus carmenque diiudicat*]. But those of the class which is dependent upon instruments and who spend their entire effort there—such as kitharists and those who prove their skill [*artificium*] on the organ and other musical instruments—are excluded from comprehension of musical knowledge [*a musica scientiae intellectu seiuncti sunt*]. . . . The second class of those practicing music is that of the poets [*genus poetarum*], a class led to song not so much by thought and reason [*speculatione ac ratione*] as by a certain natural instinct [*naturali quodam instinctu*]. For this reason this class, too, is separated from music [*a musica segregantur*]. The third class is that which acquires an ability for judging [*iudicandi*]. . . . That person is a musician [*musicus*] who exhibits the faculty of forming judgments according to speculation or reason.[2]

The two first classes belong to fairly disreputable people. Almost animals, if one believes Saint Augustine in his *De Musica*.[3]

Before this categorical classification, though, it is indeed on the basis of a fiction, a fable transmitted to medieval theoreticians by Boethius that a true division [*partage*] between (musical) *thinking* [*pensée*] and the *weighing* [*pesée*] (of bodies) was instituted.[4] It is out of a terrifying background noise, a crash of strikes of hammers, that the organized and policed edifice of the first Western musical system was raised or erected. At least that is its founding myth, taken up and hammered in over and over again for centuries.

Here then is Pythagoras, the first hero of this fable, of this fabulous genealogy:

> He [Pythagoras] put no credence in human ears [*nullis humanis auribus credens*], which are subject to change [*permutantur*], in part through nature, in part by external circumstance, and undergo changes caused by age. Nor did he devote himself to instruments [*nullis etiam deditus instrumentis*], in conjunction with which much inconstancy and uncertainty often arise [*multa varietas atque inconstantia*]. When you wish to examine strings [*nervos aspicere*], for example, more humid air may deaden the pulsation, or drier air may excite it. . . . Pythagoras was seeking a way to acquire through reason [*ratione*], unfalteringly and consistently [*firmiter et constanter*], a full knowledge of the criteria for consonances [*momenta consonantiarum*]. In the meantime, by a kind of divine will, while passing the workshop of blacksmiths [*fabrorum officinas*], he overheard [*exaudit*] the beating of hammers [*pulsos malleos*] somehow emit a single consonance from differing sounds [*ex diversis sonis unam quodam modo concinentiam personare*]. Thus in the presence of what he had long sought, he approached the activity spellbound [*adtonitus accessit ad opus*]. Reflecting for a time, he decided that the strength of the men hammering caused the diversity of sounds, and in order to prove this more clearly, he commanded them to exchange hammers among themselves. But the property of sounds did not rest in the muscles of the men; rather, it followed the exchanged hammers. When he had observed this, he examined the weight of the hammers. There happened to be five hammers, and those which sounded together the

> consonance of the diapason [that is, the octave] were found to be double in weight [in a relation of 2:1].[5]

This is how, from the most primitive percussion that exists, Pythagoras the philosopher is said to have brought about the emergence of the luminous speculation of musical intervals and harmonious proportions Five centuries after Boethius, one finds the same fable once again under the pen of the monk Guido of Arezzo, the inventor of modern solmization around the year 1000. The fable has kept all the characteristics of its earlier version, but it has grown somewhat more dramatic:

> When a certain great philosopher, Pythagoras, happened to be taking a walk, he came to a workshop in which five hammers were beating on one anvil. Amazed at their sweet concord [*concordiam*], the philosopher drew near and, expecting at first that the basis of the variety of sound and its harmony [*modulationis*] lay in the differences of the hands of the workmen, he exchanged the hammers among them. But after this was done, its quality of sound followed each hammer. So he removed from the others one that was discordant [a slight variation from Boethius's canonical version] and weighed the rest, and, in wondrous manner, by God's will, they weighed the first with twelve, the second with nine, the third with eight, and the fourth with six, of I know not what units of weight. Thus he learned that the science [*scientiam*] of music depended upon numerical ratios and comparisons [*in numerorum proportione et collatione*]. . . . What more? The renowned Pythagoras first arranged the monochord, ordering the notes by means of the aforesaid intervals. Since this monochord constitutes not a trivial but a diligently revealed knowledge of our art, it has pleased wise men in general. Up to this day our science has gradually increased and grown in strength, with

> that same Teacher bringing light to the darkness of human affairs whose supreme wisdom flourishes through all the ages. Amen.[6]

It is remarkable that the founding myth of Western musical knowledge also immediately includes an instrument that is not one: The *monochord*, with its single string stretched over a piece of wood and endowed with a mobile bridge, is a kind of *sound ruler* that, for a long time, will only be used to demonstrate the system of proportions and consonances. It's an instrument for teaching and for calculations; music is not *made* with it. It's an *indicator* that only indicates without playing.[7]

To invent this strange instrument, this monster or demonstrator represented by a *purely theoretical musical instrument*, Pythagoras had to run the gamut through the whole register of extant matters. As if it were to more easily forget them, as if he wanted to erase them by incorporating them into the systematic corpus of his speculation without bodies. In effect, after the episode with the blacksmith, the philosopher goes home. And there, returned to himself, in the element of knowledge, he proceeds as follows:

> First, he attached corresponding weights [*pondera*] to strings [*nervis*] and discerned by ear their consonances [*consonantias*]; then, he applied the double and mean and fitted other ratios [*proportiones*] to lengths of pipes [*longitudine calamorum*]. He came to enjoy a most complete assurance [*integerrimam fidem*] through the various experiments. By way of measurement, he poured ladles of corresponding weights into glasses, and he struck [*percutiens*] these glasses—set in order according to various weights—with a rod of copper or iron, and he was glad to have found nothing at variance. Thus led, he turned to length and thickness of strings [*nervis*], that he might test further. And

in this way he found the rule [*regulam*, with the double sense of the norm and the wooden measuring stick the monochord is], about which we shall speak later. . . . This kind of rule is tantamount to such fixed and enduring inquiry [*inspectio*] that no researcher [*inquirentem*] would be misled by dubious evidence.[8]

Once the rule has been established and constructed, one can forget the instruments or matters from which it had had to be painfully extracted. Music and *musicus* are now at home in the measured realm of the monochord, that sound ruler. If others continue to strike or bang, it's no longer their problem.

Starting with this moment, the chaste hand of the medieval musicus will in effect have to stop playing. It will have to touch nothing. It will at most be allowed to practice the aerial gestures of chironomy (when it directs choirs or singers from afar), but it will no longer be allowed to be in vibrant contact with sound matter. It will not be allowed to weigh its weight on skins, on bows that rub, or on levers that strike. It even becomes, ideally, a kind of theoretical instrument, as is attested by the so-called Guidonian hand (from the name of Guido of Arezzo, its supposed inventor). Here is one of them—

—that has become properly *monstrous* from demonstrating so many signs. It is an excrescence that does not play but that is contemplated as one would a painting. Or a ruler.[9]

On the other side of things, among those excluded from the theoretical corpus, among those *Musikanten* pilloried with their thundering bodies, percussion and percussionists will be notably demonic since they produce neither notes nor proportions, but only sound or noise. *Ich pauck und pfeyff euch allen her rin / Hintten in dye helle meyn*, said one devil from a German wood engraving to the damned:[10] "I drum and blow all of you / back there in my inferno."

There are thousands of ways to master bodies. They can be unmentioned or reduced to silence. They can also be covered with words or notes, tattooed with marks.

CHAPTER 4 Touch-ups, or The Return of Bodies

Waiting.

Waiting for the later touch-ups to this venerable corpus, waiting for the discrete subversions or revolutions thanks to which the world of music will once again be populated by bodies.

One has to wait a long time. One has to wait all the way up until the sixteenth century before seeing a veritable breach opened up in the confrontation between the pious *musicus* and the diabolic instrumentalists.

In a book published in Basel in 1511 under the title *Musica getutscht*, a certain Sebastian Virdung will have sketched out a first step beyond the inheritance transmitted by Boethius.[1] One can say without exaggerating that, after a millenary exile, it is in this work that musical instruments regain their rights in musical knowledge. They begin to return to populate discourses and treatises.

It is thus a new fiction, one that constructs other bodies, that begins here. But this inaugural moment is not pure; it has a hard time breaking away from the ancient erasure of bodies, and it cannot do so without a certain amount of rhetorical acrobatics.

One must in effect recall that this erasure was sustained by the allegorical disguising of bodies, by their fabulous emblematic figuration.

A piece of writing widely cited in the Middle Ages, the "Letter to Dardanus," long attributed to Saint Jerome, is burgeoning with allegorizing interpretations of the instruments mentioned in the Bible (particularly in Psalm 150 and in Daniel 3:5). This is so much the case that these biblical instruments live their own lives as theological symbols, completely detached from organological reality. Of the cithara mentioned in Psalm 43 ("Upon the harp will I praise thee, O God my God!"), the "Letter to Dardanus" gives the following exegesis: "It possesses a triangular form comparable to that of the letter *delta*, representing faith in the Holy Trinity."[2] In the same way, speaking of the psaltery, the Pseudo Jerome is not content to attribute its ten strings and its square shape to a spiritual signification ("The Church with its ten laws repressing all heresy," "the four gospels"); it even dispossesses the musician's gesture of its sound effects: "Through the indication of the pulse of the hands from below to above, one signifies that one is resuscitating from the infernos for the realm of the heavens."

This then is the epistle to which Virdung continues to refer in his treatise written in the form of a dialogue between "Andreas" and "Sebastian" and illustrated by many engravings. The mention of the "Letter to Dardanus" is first confided to the voice of Andreas (who is described—and I'll be coming back to this—as *musicus*) when he speaks of certain instruments called "Hieronymic" (from the name of Saint Jerome):

> *A[ndreas]:* When I obtained the works of St. Jerome [*opera sancti Hieronimi*], I found a treatise therein that the holy father wrote to Dardanus [*ad Dardanum*]—in the sixty-first

> letter—about the kinds of Music [*de generibus Musicorum*], [with] many more unusual shapes or forms of instruments and with many more unusual names other than [those] you have given to the instruments of the present day. . . . *Se[bastian]:* I would certainly like to see them, even more . . . to hear them, and most of all, to know what they represented; because whatever Jerome wrote about things, it always had to have a second, spiritual meaning. (111)

However, and whatever else he may say about it to keep up appearances, this allegorical or spiritual sense is far from being what interests Sebastian. Of the cithara, he contents himself with comparing the respective merits of "old and new harps"; the new ones "are also far superior in resonance, and they are made more artfully and beautifully in form for their use—for learning and playing them" (113). It is obvious: The delta shape barely has any importance in and of itself; what matters, beyond or beneath the allegory, is if it is apt to be played. The square formed by the ancient psaltery also does not interest Sebastian, who dismisses symbolic considerations in favor of a hypothesis on the properly organological history of the instrument:

> *Se.* I have never seen the psaltery that is still in use in a form other than triangular. But I believe and am of the opinion that the virginal was first thought to be made from the psaltery, so that nowadays it is touched and struck with keys and is made with quill feathers. (113)

It is as if musical instruments, once they have been detached from their mythical or biblical origin, started to form ties of filiation among themselves. Among the kinds of bodies that they are—the virginal descending from the psaltery like some organic bodies give birth to others. Once their history and genesis is no longer propped onto a meaning that is beyond them, the bodies described and represented by Virdung free themselves from their allegorical finery. And the possibility of Diderot's crazy fiction begins to open, the one d'Alembert can only acquiesce to in the *Conversation*: "I see," he was saying. "Thus if this sensitive and animated clavichord were endowed with the further powers of feeding and reproducing itself, it would live and engender on its own, or with its female, little living and resonating clavichords."[3] Yet parallel to this self-reproductive autophony, announcing the lineage of Steinway without Glenn, sonorous bodies are also exposed to being *touched, body to body*.

CHAPTER 5 Idiotisms, or The Dialect of Bodies

The *Musica getutscht* (an old spelling for *gedutscht*, or "put into German"—but in my ears, the word cannot help referring to an art of tact), this incredibly risky treatise for its time, presents itself as a dialogue between two characters: "Herr Bastian is welcomed by Andreas Silvanus, the musician," as we read in the preface-dedication.[1] Andreas is thus explicitly described as *musicus*, whereas Bastian (also spelled Sebastian[us]) has an obvious kinship with the treatise's author, Sebastian Virdung.

Their dialogue opens under the sign of a kind of prohibition. And Bastian seems to want to make sure he can transgress it with no risk:

> *A[ndreas]*: I pray you, tell me where you have been for so long. *Se[bastian]:* I have researched, investigated, and made discoveries about that [subject in pursuit of] which I have been wandering about for a long time. *A*: What is it [you have learned]? *Se*: About theoretical, practical, and instrumental music. *A*: I have been well aware that for a long time you have occupied yourself with preparing something new and unusual, but I did not know what it was. So, unless you are keeping it as your own personal

secret, I would like to ask you to tell me about it and to show it to me. *Se*: I would be most favorably inclined to grant you this request—and even larger ones—*as long as it were to bring me no disadvantage*. *A*: Dear friend, by [my] faith I tell you, *it shall be without any detriment to you whatsoever*. (100, emphasis mine)

Apparently, (Se)bastian is worried that what he has to say will be detrimental. And one can understand, so much does his discourse imply a gripping reversal of the musicus and his knowledge. In effect, if the educational scene in dialogue being prepared here is approximately molded on categories inherited from Boethius (it is still a question of theoretical, practical, and instrumental music), the way it is articulated inverts the established hierarchy: It is indeed Andreas, the *musicus*, who will be regularly placed in the position of the *ignorant person* faced with one who knows instruments and how they are played; this is so much the case that, when reading a passage from the dialogue where Andreas is dispossessed of all knowledge, one understands not only (Se)bastian's scruples but also Virdung's need to hide behind a fictive double who states what the author can only countersign in an underhanded way:

A: . . . But, I beg you, tell me how I can learn to play the instruments. Do they all have a similar principle, so that were I to learn to play wind instruments, I would then also know how to play the lute, [the] organ, or other stringed instruments in exactly the same way? *Se*: All instruments of Music as a whole are not very different when it comes to melody that is written down in notes, and whoever knows how to sing these [notes] can very easily learn to play them exactly the same on all instruments, and this [kind of] person needs no other rule. But for the others, [those] who are

> not able to sing [from notes], for them a method [*modus*] has been devised—tablature—to teach them how to learn the instruments separately, according to the type and properties of each individual instrument. *A*: I too cannot sing anything [from notes], but I do have a strong desire to learn [to play] the instruments. Could you teach me [how to play] wind instruments, [how] to strike [the] lute, or [how to play the] organ, without [teaching me] to sing? *Se*: I cannot teach you [how to play an instrument] entirely satisfactorily without [teaching you] to sing. You must learn to understand at least something of what the system is all about. At the very least you must learn to know the notes and the keys and to call them by their names. (120, translation slightly modified)

What could the knowledge of a *musicus* who knows next to nothing be worth? That he is unable to play instruments might be fine: For a *musicus*, this ignorance was appropriate. But he also does not know how to sing, no more than he knows the names of the notes. One wonders what might remain from the old hierarchy inherited from Boethius.

There does at least remain, indirectly, an opposition between song (in the singular) and instruments (in the plural): between, on the one hand, the voice that knows music *in general* and, on the other hand, digital or mechanical practical knowledge that remains prisoner to the *particularities* of the organ, lute, or flute. As Sebastian explains here, what allows one to go from one instrument to another, to reduce the diversity of their mechanisms in order the better to master them *all*, is song: the knowledge or reason of the voice, its *logos*. Tablature, however, essentially destined for the fingers of those who do not know how to sing, remains widely prisoner to the dialectal and digital characteristics of one instrument over another. (Sebastian is very clear on this point: "Because of this difference or distinction [between the instruments], there was invented and discovered *for each its own tablature* that is suitable and practical for learning" [121, emphasis mine].)

In other words, tablature is, potentially, a means of addressing the ignorant or the *idiots* in music (among whom Andreas the musicus can be counted) to teach an instrumental touch that will remain irremediably idiomatic, or *idiotic*, within a general musical language accessible only to the voice.[2] Tablature is the domain of the *idiot's idiolect*.

Besides the idea of a filiation from instrument to instrument without going through a legitimating ontotheology, it is indeed the tablatures given by Virdung that give his treatise its modernity.[3] They opened a possibility theretofore unheard-of in the organological corpus, that of a laborious manual apprenticeship, with step-by-step progress, or rather finger-by-finger. This is how Sebastian teaches flute to Andreas, who has grown mute and fumbling *on the body of the instrument*:

> *Se*: . . . And since you have eight holes on the recorder, we will therefore take just the first eight numerals for this purpose, and [standing] for the lowest two holes (which, after all, are counted as only one, and on which the little finger belongs) we will put a numeral that represents "one" in numbers, like this: 1. [Standing] For the second hole, on which the ring finger belongs, we will put a numeral that represents "two" in numbers, like this: 2. [And so on, in just as repetitive a manner, up until 8]. (170)

The result of this digital and properly *idiotic* didactics is that musical theory is transferred onto the body of the instrument itself, from which it becomes difficult to *abstract* it. The flute represented in the engraving is covered with numbers, as the fingers of the Guidonian hand were with letters. And the possibility of *blind* learning that thus opens, using tables and rules inscribed *on the very body of the instrument*, finds a kind of echo in what Sebastian states elsewhere of the lute: "I hear that there was a blind man born in Nuremberg and buried in Munich, named Meister Conrad from Nuremberg, who . . . directed that the entire alphabet be written [crosswise] on the five courses and *on the seven frets of the neck*" (156, emphasis mine).

This indicates just how much the support of mnemonic signs that was the (Guidonian) hand hands things off to the stick, thanks to the idiotism of tablatures. And what then begins is a new *effiction* of sonorous bodies whose consequences are huge. What is lost and engulfed in it is the unity of a corpus gauged on knowledge and on obliviousness to weight. What opens up within it, at the risk of falling, is what we will see is the occasion, the chance for a question infinitely asked and constantly to be negotiated: the question of *ligatures* [*liaisons*] from body to body.

CHAPTER 6 **Monk, a Legend**

Insert here, skipping over eras and as if it were an aside, his name, his legend.

The legend of the one who, perhaps more than all the others, delivered himself body and soul *to the occasion*.

I would certainly not say that he *grabbed* the occasion. He put himself *at risk* in it, put himself at stake.

Monk—Thelonious Sphere Monk—is probably the musician who, more than any other, experienced distance. The distance from himself to himself that he constantly experienced and made resonate *on a keyboard*.

This is what we hear when he plays alone. His left hand moves imperturbably in old stride style: a bass note on the first beat, a chord stuck onto the second, and so on and so forth, infinitely, in tireless step. It's what jazzmen call in French "*la pompe*," or pumping. While his right hand is by turns agile, jerky, dissonant, fantastical, insistent, repetitive, angular, even voluntarily clumsy [*maladroite*] and *gauche*.... Always unpredictable, it seems to ignore the other one, the left hand, the one over there that remains so regular and rigid and straight [*droite*], almost indifferent.

Between them, there is more than just stylistic dissonance: a whole world. An attentive witness—a pianist who has listened to him a lot—has written, "The left hand was classic, and the right was modern. Take away the left hand and there would be the Monk of twenty years later. Remove the right, and we would be back to the jazz of twenty years earlier."[1] If I count right, that makes forty years between these two playing hands. Forty years' distance, here, now, in the same instant. And forty years, in the history of jazz, is already quite a lot.

I am sometimes even tempted to imagine that, between Monk's two hands, there may be centuries. Perhaps millennia, between his occasionally very awkward [*gauche*] right hand and his always straight [*droite*] left hand.

Many are the pianists who recorded Monk's themes and thus contributed to his legend. Almost all, whatever they may say or do, transform them into something *pretty*. Something harmonious and unified. Under others' fingers, what passed *between* Monk's hands seems to get lost: They play as if they were only one man, only one body.

There is, perhaps, one exception: Bill Evans, in his solo recording of *Bemsha Swing*. Which is in fact not exactly a solo, even if no one else is named on the jacket. The album is called *Conversations with Myself*: It is indeed a dialogue, but from him to him. Bill Evans used all the resources of phonography: He recorded himself on a first track, and then, listening to himself, he recorded himself again on another one. He dialogues and converses with himself, as he explains on the notes that accompany the record:

> I remember that in recording the selections, as I listened to the first track while playing the second, and the first two while playing the third, the process involved was an artifi-

cial duplication of simultaneous performance in that each track represented a musical mind responding to another musical mind or minds. The argument that the same mind was involved in all three performances could be advanced, but I feel that this is not quite true.[2]

Listening to himself play at the same time as himself, he wonders. He hears himself, he answers himself, but he hesitates. Apparently, it's definitely him; it is indeed to images of his sonorous body that he speaks in the mirror of the recording. But these images are *not exactly* him. They tremble. This is why he sometimes seems to think that there are three of him, three bodies that do not make a whole: "I feel that the music here has more the quality of a 'trio' than a solo effort," he says before opting immediately for the contrary, before arguing that, once everything is weighed out, in the end there is only one and the same body with itself: "Yet I hesitate to state this recorded result is identical to trio performance. . . . It is in the end still the product of one subject."

This hesitation, which can be heard in an incredible way in his playing between the tracks, was also Monk's. Except that Monk did not take recourse to any apparatus or studio technology; it's all alone, naked in front of his piano, *in his purest state* [*son plus simple appareil*] that he himself became the stake of a postsynchronization of the self.

Monk, they say, had imagined a strange apparatus when, as a very young boy, he was learning the piano: "To better study the position of his fingers . . . , he installed a mirror above his piano and played with his eyes set on the ceiling."[3]

As we know, Monk wore a ring on his left-hand ring finger inscribed with the letters M, O, N, and K. His ring spells out his patronymic; it renames him and thus contributes to his renown.

Monk, like a monk in the church. Backwards, it reads *know*; *monknow*: horizontal and vertical mirror, a palindrome or little anagram of which he was apparently very fond.

Monk, I tell myself, could therefore have been a monk. And have wanted to devote his life to the knowledge of a *musicus*.

Were I to know nothing of his music and of his singular relation to the piano, were I reduced, like I am for medieval monks, to speculating on iconography that shows him with his ring on his finger, with this motto inscribed backward in his name, Monk might appear to me as a strange, ancient figure, a latecomer to the twentieth century. Like someone who would have made the following, very ancient statement his own: "A musician is someone who possesses the ability to judge according to speculation and reason." The one who *knows*.

Of course, since I have often watched and listened to him, since I still today so often perceive in my phonographic or filmic archives that surprising division that crosses through him and puts him at a sonorous distance from himself, I know this isn't true: Reason certainly did desert the keyboard where Monk feels and brings me to feel intervals whose *reason cannot be given*, so much are they incarnated in a body that is far from being *one*. And which probably isn't, or at least is not merely, *his* body.

Something of the ancient knowledge still resonates, from far away, in his name—and even in that strange second name (Sphere) that one might believe fallen here below from the *musica mundana*, from that "music of spheres" that, in Boethius, was the reason for the system, for the *corpus*, the reason of musical reason.

And yet Monk, in many ways, is much closer to the others, to those that the history of Western music had to start by forgetting. In order to start. On the keyboard, Monk strikes and hits when he plays: "Sometimes he'd hit a chord on the keyboard, then immediately raise his arms as if he had received a jolt. Then he'd stare at the piano with a perplexed air . . . as if the piano played all by itself."[4] This shows just how much so many of the characteristics of the archaic blacksmiths mix together here, with their prophetic and prosthetic idiotism that waited so long for its occasion, for its chance.

Monk, we might think, did not *know* what he was doing very well. It played all by itself, with him or without him.

But perhaps he knew very well what he was doing, but with an entirely different form of knowledge than that of the *musicus*. As has sometimes been noted, even if Monk seems to make his piano speak "in an unpredictable way," even if he seems to play "by inventing rules as he went along," there is always, "even when hesitating . . . a magnificent self-confidence."[5] What is this hesitating self-confidence or this self-confident hesitation that, apparently, has little to do with Pythagoras's "complete assurance" [*integerrimam fidem*] in the fable? What is this other knowledge that Monk, all while hammering away at his keyboard, would find pleasure in seeing reflected and thrown over, starting with his name on the ring, in the black and shiny lacquer mirror of the piano?

Let us say for the moment that Monk evokes or *conjures*, at the very same time he perverts, the reflection of a powerful form of reason hailing from the dawn of ages. He is playing with its shadow, its ghost. I can only offer here, as is, the gripping hypothesis of someone who has listened to Monk very closely. Speaking of the rings, and particularly the one that vaunts knowledge, he suggests that Monk wore the rings "on purpose to prevent himself from playing."[6]

Monk's hand indeed bears signs. They are letters that, even if they do not compose a scale as they do for the *musicus* (the French word for scale, *gamme*, comes from the *gamma* that figured on the first phalanx of the thumb of the Guidonian hand), inscribe an almost common proper name: *Monk*, a monk.

Nonetheless, under the appearance of a musical monk, Monk will perhaps have been a devil, for not only does he have nothing chaste or measured about him, not only does his right hand strike the strongest dissonances, but it is also his entire body that one sometimes hears on certain record tracks. For example, his claws. His hands, says his biographer, "were more like palms divided into five parts. Each fingertip seemed to be all nail which seemed alone to cover the whole last phalanx, an almost vegetal result of this subdivision."[7] Monk is a particularly vivacious plant whose body seems to ramify in unexpected ways, to such an extent that sometimes "his extraordinary nails . . . had to be cut during a recording session," as was the case during a 1971 session in London whose archive I so love to listen to, over and over again:[8] One hears the noise these claws make as they rub up against the keyboard, as if Monk were accompanied by a guero, that instrument in the shape of a comb that you scrape.

And on top of it all, Monk dances. With his little pointed beard and his strange hat, he often gets up from the keyboard to step out with a few steps between danse macabre and Sabbath. Or else, when he stays seated to play, one sees his foot—that one readily imagines forked under his shoes—keeping time *without touching the ground*. In a kind of pulsating levitation that, assuredly, has something supernatural about it.[9]

Monk, who magnificently seized the chances of idiotism in music (sometimes allowing himself to give himself up to them), became Monk, apparently, only thanks to a certain *autophony*[10] whose traces we've already noted, particularly when he perplexedly contemplates his piano that seems to play by itself.

"We know," states his biographer, that "he started off with the trumpet but dropped it immediately when the family purchased a player piano. The five-year-old was fascinated by the keys that moved by themselves." Like other jazzmen, like Art Tatum, who "learned to play, adapting player-piano music written for four hands into music for two hands," Monk becomes the pianist he is only through the trickery of *autophones*. He learns to play, he learns *his* playing and *his* body-to-body experience [*corps à corps*], by furthering what is played without him. In an ever recommenced hand-to-hand struggle [*corps à corps*], he ties and binds together [*relie*] the *membra disjecta* of numerous mechanical hands whose interruptions he watches, fascinated, stupefied. Idiotic.

CHAPTER 7 **Traces of Fingers**

Linking [*lier*] the keys, linking the fingers and hands, but also linking oneself (to) oneself in a phrase that is *one*, that makes up a body and constructs the sonorous unity of "my" body: Starting in Virdung's era and continuing until Monk's legend, this question remains open. It is even gaping wide.

And in this question we find the possibility for a reinvention or a reinscription of bodies on the basis of the melee of their bodily struggles [*corps à corps*], against the backdrop of idiotism.

The question of ligature [*liaison*] was probably not posed, or at least not in the same terms, for the first keyboards that were activated by the whole palm of the hand (in his 1650 *Musurgia universalis*, the theoretician Athanase Kircher still speaks of *palmulas* for the keys of an organ). In antiquity, these first keyboards were effectively applied to instruments—hydraulic organs—that must have looked more like forges than typewriters. One can get an idea of this *palm playing* [*jeux de paumes*] by

observing certain illuminations or illustrations of medieval manuscripts.[1]

Yet starting with the era of Virdung, the keyboardist's fingers have begun their emancipation, unlinking themselves from his hand or his palm: The keys of the organs or clavichords represented in *Musica getutscht* have apparently become exclusively digital.

There is no doubt more than a coincidence between the organic unlinking [*déliaison*]—the reinvention of the keyboardist's hand that finds itself metamorphosed by the new growth of five unprecedented branches—and the distances and abysses dug out by the idiotism of the sonorous body delivered to itself from its separation from a theoretico-allegorical corpus that, until then, found itself unified in one way or another.

It is nonetheless still the case that this era of delinking [*déliaison*] and of the thrust of the fingers' independence movement is also, more or less, that of the first archived indications as to the manner of *fingering* the keyboard: It is only from the beginning of the sixteenth century that the *tangible* traces of concrete digital movements have come to us, traces that record the articulatory movements of the phalanges and that allows them to be deciphered. These *traces of fingers* are in a way the maculatures of keyboardists—certainly dirty things in comparison to the *musicus's* chaste hand. By opening up the possibility of reading [*lire*] the fingers, they also cause the correlative emergence of the question: How are we to *link* [*lier*] them?

(Between linking [*lier*] and reading [*lire*], there is in fact an anagrammatic relation that is perhaps not foreign to the one we saw in Monk's fingers).

Reading the fingers, then. Following each one of them, one by one, in their agile or groping movements on keyboards.

And wondering each time, when faced with fingerprints we keep of past body-to-body experiences, what was in play on the keys.

Deciphering *à la lettre* the construction in act of bodies that today are lost but that survive in gestures as long-lasting as ghosts: This is the fantasy the keyboardist archives are not far from allowing us to access.

Yet one must specify that tablature, which delegates to the fingers what was formerly reserved for the *logos*, does not necessarily allow us to follow manual gymnastics with any precision. The tablature for the lute given by Virdung indeed indicates, and now without recourse to prerequisite knowledge, the *place* the fingers will come to occupy on the neck. But it does not describe or archive *the movements of the fingers themselves*. In the same way, when later tablatures for keyboards (like Juan Bermudo's in his 1555 *Declaraciòn de instrumentos musicales*) number the keys from low to high pitch, these numbers certainly allow someone to play without knowing (anything), like some kind of slightly Monkian Andreas, but they never say whether it is the thumb, index, or other finger that comes to occupy the prescribed key.

The oldest trace of *effective* digital movements (movements that have been effectively registered as such) seems to be the handwritten copy of a *Fundamentbuch* by the German organist Hans Buchner: It dates from around 1520, that is, slightly after Virdung's treatise. The work by the Italian keyboardist Girolamo Diruta, *Il Transilvano*, from 1593, also constitutes a remarkable document: It is probably the first to propose the theory according to which the "right" notes (in other words notes accentuated on the downbeat) must be confided to the "right" fingers, that is to the index and ring fingers.[2]

We can thus see the progressive constitution, starting with the idiotic space opened by the tablatures, of traces of *finger-*

ings. Documents recording the ways fingers touch. But we have to wait until François Couperin and his wonderful *Art of Playing the Harpsichord*[3] for these traces to begin to gather together and form a veritable version of a *digital archive* in whose historical thickness we will be able to distinguish several types of bodies at play.

Couperin begins by numbering the fingers. By attributing numbers and signs to them. This is not in any way the same operation as the Guidonian hand: Here, the fingers are not *covered up* with letters or numbers; nothing is masked or hidden—one counts *with* them rather than *on* them; in the final analysis, it is even perhaps they, and they alone, that count.

There are five of them. At least for the moment. Five on each hand. Couperin counts them, on the left (from 5 to 1) and on the right (from 1 to 5); he *digitalizes* them: He translates them into digits.

And especially, as far as the tablature is concerned, Couperin takes one further step: He does not simply use these finger-digits to propose a representation of music that would substitute for score notation; he *superposes* over the score in notes a kind of score numbered for the fingers: We start to see the *digits* indicating a little finger (5) or a thumb (1) proliferate, in short veritable fingerprints above or beneath the notes. (The illustration in chapter 9—fingering indications left by Carl Philipp Emanuel Bach, which we will discuss a bit later—gives a good idea of this co-presence of a score with staves and a digital score.)

This is why the digits are no longer only there, like the tablatures, to *replace* the score for ignorant people like Andreas: They are no longer a reductive last resort. On the contrary, they *add* something through their superscription that the notes could not say. This, I think, is how one has to understand Couperin when, in his preface, he declares:

> The method that I present here is unique, and has no connection with the tablature which is but the science of numbers. Here I deal with all matters regarding fine harpsichord playing (by proven principles). . . . As there is a great distance from grammar to declamation, so there is an infinitely greater one between the tablature and good playing style.

The tablature, he basically says, was in the end perhaps nothing more than a numerology, like the abstract knowledge of the *musicus in whose place it stood.* It of course certainly sometimes indicated the position of the fingers, but it said nothing about the fingers themselves, nothing about their role and their concerted play in the *phrasing.*

In effect, the question as to how to phrase keyboard music (how to phrase oneself in it) can only be posed once any given work can tolerate several possible fingerings, which implies that, unlike the tablature that *replaces* it, any indication of fingering must be *confronted* with the score, whether in front of it or to one side of it, as one possibility among others for phrasing it. It is with fingering rather than with tablature that music for keyboard is truly enriched with a *new* dimension: that of the digital articulation of a phrase. Emancipated from their role as a *notation table,* the fingers, *untied* from the notes, add a supplementary staff to the work where several possible narratives or recitations are told for the music noted above or below.

If there is the same distance from tablature to fingering as there is from grammar to declamation, this is because we go from a form of deciphering the music to a form of *reading* it [*lire*] and of *holding it together* [*lier*].

With the underwritten or overwritten fingering, there are thus now different ways of linking (reading) [*lier (lire)*] a keyboard score; and this is why the question of ligature is posed autonomously. (When Couperin affirms that "the manner of fingering does much for good playing," one must suppose with him that it *has no other use*, that it is no longer in any case the placeholder for solfège notation.)

This is also because linking (reading) can have a history: The *choices* of fingerings will be plural (Couperin speaks of "passages in my pieces where the fingering seems ambiguous"); there will be many options, which vary with interpreters and contexts, and even with the bodies at play. The fingerings, which will now be able to come from the past or the future, will be *manners* of "declaiming" the unity of a musical phrase. And perhaps of *pronouncing* (for) the unity of bodies in music.

Couperin in fact opens up the concrete perspective of a historicity of fingering. He does this in particular when he discusses certain "ornaments used in playing" such as the "*port-de-voix*" or "appoggiatura" (39). Here we have to read Couperin right into the blindly digital details of his treatise in order to crack open a window onto the manufacture and becoming of musicking bodies that are announced in his work.

Simply stated, the "port-de-voix" is, when one goes from one note to another right next to it (*si-do*), the brief repetition of the first before the attack on the second. As the name given to this "ornament" indicates, there is a kind of *keyboard-equivalent* for the *portamento* of singers: a way of imitating, with keys that are *discrete*, and as much as is possible, their vocal way of *continuously* sliding from one note to another. The vocation of the port-de-voix is a quasi-vocal ligature on an instrument that, with its keyboard of keys, imposes disjunctions between the notes.

Yet to realize this effect, Couperin distinguishes between "old ways" and "new ways": "I have found that there are two ways to finger them," he explains. "However, in my opinion, one is preferable to the other." Couperin even claims to distinguish between the two fingerings blindly, with only his ears, "without seeing the performer's hands."

One has to make the effort, at least once, to *manually* follow the difference between the two fingerings. It's worth it because an entire digital craft allows itself to be touched with a finger. Here it is—I am miming as I read:

1. In the old way described by Couperin, it is, on the right hand, the same finger—the third, the middle one—that is charged with the task of repeating the *si* before the following finger, the ring finger, hits *do* (3–3-4, then);
2. whereas in the modern way proposed by Couperin, there is a crossing of the fingers that, at first, is surprising: the middle finger does indeed play the *si*, but it's the index that repeats it before the middle finger hits the *do* (3–2-3, then).

So much so that, on the first key (*si*), we watch the digital gymnastics of an index finger that passes *over* the middle finger (3–2), that *relays* it in order to allow it to shift to the right in order to hit the following *do*.

What, according to Couperin, is to be won from this anatomically uncomfortable crossover? Quite simply put, *ligature*: In the old fingering, the middle finger, being obliged to leave the key before returning to it "in order to re-play the little lost note" (3–3), "allows less legato" than there when it is "replaced" by the index (3–2). In other words: If, in conformity with anatomical evidence, it is the *same* finger that repeats the attack on the same key, one must raise it for a new strike, and thus *detach* the two *si* notes, whereas the new solution proposed by Couperin brings one finger to slide into the place of the other, on the same key, in order to obtain a better ligature. This is what is at stake in the crossover, in the chiasmus of fingers placed in a cross.

CHAPTER 8 Digital Rhetoric

Accent and declamation are thus played out in the fingers. There is a veritable digital *rhetoric* that, since music is also a way of saying oneself, also puts the unity of self into play. (The fingers, one could say in rhetorical terms, relay one another, give themselves over to anaphora, one taking the place of the other like the pronoun takes the place of a noun.)[1]

Now Couperin's lesson is that this unity is produced only at the cost of a certain number of reversals, contortions, crossings, or chiasmi. The ligature [*le lié*], the organic unity (of music and self) can be imagined only against the backdrop of a system of relays, substitutions, and shifts. In other words, the fingers take on postures, attitudes; they execute all kinds of figures in order, in the end, to make of and in the music that they play a beautiful body, a beautiful envelope with finely ligatured forms [*formes bien liées*]. No doubt in the hope that the phrase or the line that they articulate will allow the listener to forget their painful or twisted movements, that it will no longer say anything more than the unity or harmony of their body-to-body contact with the instrument. The rhetoric of fingers, like any rhetoric worth its name, must be effaced as such in the happy effect it produces. It has to disappear by virtue of its very elegance.

(And yet, it will never be able to disappear completely, since Couperin claims to hear it even without seeing the body or the fingers.)

Classical treatises in rhetoric speak of discourses in terms of *figures*: as if, like a body, discourses had a silhouette and took on certain postures, more or less expressive attitudes. This analogy is constant at least since Cicero ("figures the Greeks called *schemata*, as if they were 'attitudes' of discourse," he says in his *De Oratore*, XXV, 83) and right up to the work of César Chesneau Du Marsais, a contemporary of Couperin, who writes:

> *Figure*, in the proper sense, is the exterior form of a body. All bodies are extended; yet beyond this property of being extended, they each still have their particular figure and form which makes it so that each body appears to our eyes as different from another body; the same is true of figurative expressions; they first allow what one thinks to be known; they first have that general property that is appropriate to all phrases and all assemblages of words, and which consists in signifying something thanks to the grammatical construction; yet in addition figurative expressions have yet another particular modification proper to them, and it is thanks to this particular modification that one makes each kind of figure into a separate type.[2]

The figures of a discourse are therefore the way this verbal body is phrased by taking on forms and varied organic envelopes. Or else by turning and returning itself in all directions, as is the case in particular of figures that affect words:

> These figures are called *tropes*, from the Greek *tropos, convérsio*, whose root is *trepo, verto, I turn*. They are called this

> because when one takes a word in the figurative sense, one turns it, in a manner of speaking, in order to make it mean what it does not mean in the proper sense: *sails* in the proper sense does not mean *ships*.[3]

Like the keyboard player's articulations, words offer themselves to twists and turns. And on this basis it is tempting to imagine a general rhetoric, a *tropics*, where everything would turn, hands like the parts of sentences, the fingers of Couperin or Monk like the words of Corneille or La Bruyère or the Bible (to stay with Du Marsais's favorite examples).

But by attempting to make fingers *speak* in this way, do we not once again run the risk of dispossessing them of their idioms and of inscribing them once again into a logic or *logos* that erases what is proper to them?

CHAPTER 9 Ablations and Grafts (Too Many Fingers)

In fact, there are at least two rhetorics of fingers on the keyboard.

The first, overjoyed at having numbered the fingers and counting with their finite number (five on each hand), gives an inventory of their postures, their *figures*, and assigns them to a sense, to an effect of phrasing. This rhetoric is content with the count and proceeds to construct a diction.

On the contrary, the second, attentive to the intuitions of many keyboardists interested in the *becoming* of the fingers—in their lives, necroses, and rebirths—would allow the phalanges and members to proliferate without being assured of the count, at the cost of giving up on diction.

The first takes stock of the fingers—the bodies—by attributing them to the account of a construction of musical sense in the manner in which an "I" plays. The second simply opens the infinite construction of their multiplying.

It is this second rhetoric, I believe, that brings Carl Philipp Emmanuel Bach to state, about Couperin and his other predecessors, that "sometimes they had too many fingers [*zu viel Finger*]," whereas he and his contemporaries have "too few" of them. And this is why, in all seriousness, he was able to form the project of seeking out the "main ways we comfortably obtain in a manner of speaking as many fingers as we need [*wodurch wir bequem so viel Finger gleichsam kriegen als wir brauchen*]."[1]

We must take Bach at his word when he speaks of the fingers and their properly *indefinite* number. This is not an easy thing to do when common sense (that of the first rhetoric) would have us believe that the keyboardist is already endowed with a constituted hand and body before sitting down in front of the keys. For one English translator of Bach, at any rate, the idea that a hand-on-a-keyboard can, unlike other hands, have more than five fingers remains unreadable: In his English translation (which is certainly less of an affront to anthropological reason), Bach is looking for nothing but the means "whereby we can extend the range" covered by the fingers.

But if we follow Bach literally, the keyboardist's hand has the particularity of demanding that it be *reinvented* every time. To my knowledge, Bach is the first to say in an explicit way that, on keyboard instruments (harpsichord, clavichord, or fortepiano), *there is no natural position of the fingers*:

> The fingering [*die Setzung der Finger*] is, on most instruments, established [*festgesetzt*] in a way by their natural constitution: for keyboards, it seems on the contrary to be the most arbitrary [*am willkürlichsten*] to the extent that the position of the keys is constituted so that they can be lowered by any finger whatsoever.[2]

In other words: Whereas the flute or the clarinet, for example, demand as many fingers as there are holes to be covered up in order to emit a given note, and these instruments (and many others) prescribe or preinscribe the position of each finger of the two hands onto their body,[3] the keyboard, on the contrary, can in principle be played by any given number of fingers (between one and ten, perhaps even more), used in whatever order. It all depends on *what* is being played on it, and *how*.

Apparently, if you execute polyphonic music on a keyboard, you will have less choice as to the fingering; the greater the number of fingers simultaneously set into play on the keyboard, the more fixed and frozen is their order on the keyboard. Bach writes:

> Our predecessors, who were more devoted to harmony than to melody, as a result most often played in a fully polyphonic way [*vollstimmig*]. We will see in what follows that, because this kind of motif can be made only in one way and hardly allow for possible variants, each finger, in a manner of speaking, finds its place indicated for it.[4]

In contrast, in the "melodic passages" [*melodischen Passagien*], the use of fingers "is much more arbitrary." Thus, for Bach, a rising scale in C-major played with only one hand can be fingered in three different ways; the two hands therefore offer six possibilities, among which "none is to be rejected."

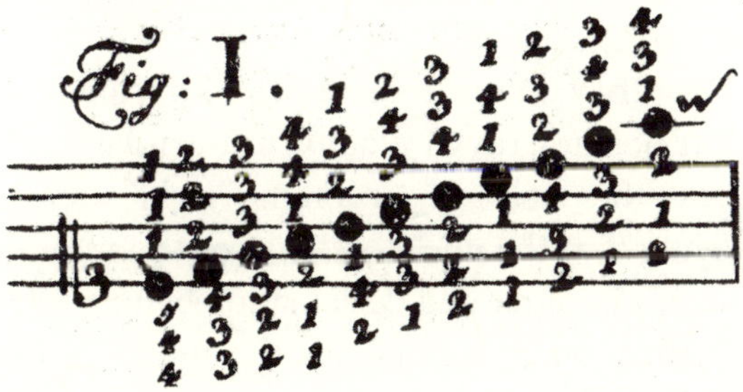

Along with Bach, we can draw two consequences from this example.

The first consequence is that, as the numbered sequences literally allow us to see, the keyboardist's problem is essentially that of the *multiplication of the fingers*: "With our five fingers, we can only strike five notes one after the other," so much so that, as we read, it will be necessary to find ways to obtain "as many fingers as we need." Bach counts two ways (that one finds respectively at the first and second lines of his example): the "subposition" [*Untersetzen*] of the thumb, which "passes" under the other fingers and serves as a mobile pivot for translating them onto the keyboard; and the "cover-over" [*Überschlagen*, crossing, tuilage) of the other fingers (§25). The second way is the oldest; Couperin suggested crossing as a way of obtaining better liaison; the first, which makes the other one obsolete, is promised to a fine, Romantic future (to which I'll be returning).

The second consequence is that if the ways of making the fingers proliferate are many, not all are equally worthy: They must be chosen as a function of the expression, of the way of declaiming or "saying" the music, which explains the following repeated affirmations of Bach: "There is, however, only one good way of using fingers on the keyboard" (§2); "one can absolutely not comfortably get by without the right fingers" (§7), and so on—affirmations whose source is given by the very title of the treatise (*Essay on the* True *Art of Playing Keyboard Instruments*). Despite appearances, these assertions are not in contradiction with the idea of fingering's arbitrariness; they do not come down to postulating a natural, absolute position (as Girolamo Diruta did when he spoke in his time of the "right" fingers on the "right" notes). Bach is simply saying that the *always relative* criterion of fingering is the kind of discourse and declamation being sought out. It is "taste." Thus, when he defends the intensive use of the thumb (unlike what was valid for Couperin), we understand that a veritable *reconfiguration* of the hand is under way, which adds a new finger and reestablishes its balance around it so as *to conform to a manner*:

> Anyone who does not use the thumb allows it to hang down so that it doesn't block the path; in such a configuration, even the slightest shift becomes uncomfortable because, in order to do it, the fingers must be extending and grow rigid. . . . The use of the thumb not only gives the hand *a supplementary finger*, it also provides the key for the entire possible manner of applying the fingers [*zur ganzen möglichen Applicatur*]. This main finger makes itself increasingly useful because *it maintains the suppleness of the others* by always obliging them to bend so that it can make its entry after this or that one [i.e., so that it can pass under the other fingers]. Without it, one would have to execute this through leaps and with rigid, tensed nerves, whereas it is now played, thanks to its help, *in a round, clear way*, with natural distances, and thus easily.[5]

Bach thus affords an understanding of the principle of a growth in supernumerary members; he gives the reason for them through the musical idea they serve: "Almost any new idea [*Gedanke*] demands a new fingering proper to it," he also writes.[6]

There are thus, starting with Bach, many fingers that plunge into the reasoned space of the didactics of the keyboard. But that's not all. What still awaits the fingers is hybridization with other members. Always more members, always other ones. And perhaps *for no good reason*, in absolute rupture with the first rhetoric.

CHAPTER 10 Romantic Fingers (System of Touch)

From a genetic point of view attentive to the *becoming* of fingers, the later history of keyboard fingering, its romantic history, must be understood as the pursuit and amplification of the movement begun by Carl Philipp Emmanuel Bach. It effectively brings about an *equalization* among the fingers (they must all have the same worth and equivalent strength), so much so that it makes them infinitely substitutable and easily reproduced.

One example among many others is the *Méthode des méthodes de piano* by François-Joseph Fétis,[1] whose title page underlines its "panoramic" historical synthesis:

> *Method of Methods of Piano* / or / *Treatise on the Art of playing this instrument / Based on the analysis of the best works written on this subject and particularly on the Methods* / of / *Ch. P. E. Bach, Marpurg, Türk, A. E. Müller, Dussek, Clementi, Hummel, Misters Adam, Kalkbrenner and A. Schmidt / as well as on the comparison and appreciation of the different Systems of Execution and fingering of several Famous Virtuosi / such as Misters / Chopin, Cramer, Döhler, Henselt, Liszt, Moscheles, Thalberg.*

The question of the equalization of the fingers, a sine qua non for correct execution, is articulated in a very explicit way in section 26:

> The goodness of tact or of touch, the source not only for the volume of the sound, but also of its more or less smooth quality, is the consequence of a complete liberty and independence of the fingers. The clearness of the execution can exist only if *all fingers have equal strength and suppleness.* Now, because of the anatomic conformation of the hand, the thumb and index have a lot of strength, and are independent from the other fingers, able to act with freedom without the hand being destabilized by their movements; but the other fingers do not benefit from the same advantages. The third is in a kind of dependence on the index and is less easily moved. This can be seen through the slight contraction that manifests itself in the hand while the four other fingers are kept pressed down while making this third finger move at a certain speed. The fourth and fifth fingers are in a kind of dependence on each other; the little finger in particular encounters great difficulty in moving when the four other fingers are pressed down . . . With these defects in the fingers, there is no possible correct execution. Before any further study, it is therefore indispensable to perform long exercises *to give all the fingers on both hands equal aptitude, equal suppleness, equal strength*, and perfect independence from one another.[2]

Besides this work of the standardization and normalization of the fingers (which therefore comes down to reinventing or reconfiguring a *new* hand-on-a-keyboard), one must also disarticulate the fingers from the rest of the body, in other words break their ties to the wrist, the arm, and the shoulder; this romantic operation of chiroplastic surgery continues as follows: “The attack on the keys must be done through the fingers independently of any help and any movement of the wrist” (§20); it is advised that one “isolate their mechanical articulation from any effort of the arm and shoulder” (§39); in short, one must make of the fingers a series of levers whose mechanism “must be lively, independent, and clear, like the release of a spring” (§20).

It is this perfect interchangeability and lack of tie [*déliaison*] in principle among the different fingers that allows one both to consider touch in a systematic way (it is a question of a “system of touch,” §3) and to rationalize the disposition of the fingers on the keyboard: “The difficulty of correctly *regulating the fingering* results from the fact that the number of notes that come after one another, whether rising or descending, is often greater than that of the fingers of the hand” (§40, my emphasis). As for Bach, the observation of a *lack of fingers* makes the question of fingering arise. But unlike in Bach’s *Essay*, here the fingering is theorized in a much more normative and unified way: The scale of C can no longer support three competing fingerings per hand but can admit only one (with the passage of the thumb obligatory after the middle finger, §60).

There is thus a normative fingering of reference in relation to which all the other possibilities become deviations, either because of mechanical necessity—in complex or polyphonic passages—or in view of a particular expression.[3]

In this sense, the codification that the *Method of Methods* operates over previous historical treatises bears a strong resemblance, mutatis mutandis, to that of a rhetorician such as Pierre Fontanier who, in 1818, republished Du Marsais’s *Tropes* and accompanied them with a *Reasoned Commentary*. In the same way, Fétis credits Hummel for having first collected “the diverse circumstances that can occur in the succession of fingers on a key, in order to compose a complete system of classifications" (§40). A system that, in its very terminology (as Fétis takes it up), bears striking resemblance to a reasoned treatise on digital *figures.*

Here is a small sample of the tropes that regulate the movements of romantic fingers.[4] One counts and identifies in it in particular:

1. the "*elision* of one or several fingers" (that other authors cited by Fétis name "fingering by contraction," in other words by "one's bringing two fingers far from one another on the hand together, by leaving the intermediary fingers inactive");
2. the "*substitution of fingers*" (or "changing a finger on the same key")
3. the "*alternation*," "*enlacing*," and "*crossing*" of hands
4. the "*freedoms in fingering*" (or "exceptional fingering"), in other words "the use of one and the same finger on several consecutive notes, sliding a finger from one key to another [always a black to a white], the enjambment of one finger by another, simultaneously hitting two notes with one single finger."

And so on.

It therefore seems that there are rather fewer fingers than there are for Bach, and fewer types of fingering on the Romantic keyboard. Their egalitarian normalization—which is in solidarity with a theory of the deviations that can be pictured only against a normed background—nonetheless prepares other tropes and tropics that imply other limbs.

CHAPTER 11 **Feet**

The history of the romantic foot-at-the-piano is, indeed, also the story of normalization. But before finding itself prescribed with certain codified movements, on the two or three pedals contemporary pianos still include, the pianist's foot and leg have experienced an extraordinary flowering of prostheses. It is this equipment of the foot that leads it, along with the hand, into what seems increasingly to me like an infinite tropology.

The feet have long been busy on foot mechanisms for the organ (Halberstadt's organ reproduced in Michael Praetorius's *De Organographia* dates from around 1360 and includes a *Pedal-Clavier*), yet their function cannot at first be distinguished from that of the fingers: They press down on a "pedal-key" to produce the desired note. The organist's two feet are in a way supplementary hands or toes, making the number of "fingers" increase from ten to twelve.[1]

What is actually new, however, is this "major movement of the foot" described by a journalist in 1833 in a journal called *Le Pianiste*: a movement "we can call *breathing* by comparing it to the action of the lungs in a singer."[2]

How are we to understand this shift in function of one organ to another, from the lung to the foot? What prepared for this transfer? Or what made it emerge?

We need to trace out a lineage different from the one for organ pedals, another family tree of feet. Beyond the keyboard and its keys, it is also the "organ stops" [*jeux d'orgue*] that, by moving to the clavichord and to the harpsichord, saw themselves transferred to the lower limbs. These "expression boxes" [*boîtes d'expression*] that, on the organ, allowed for the variation of timbres and nuances, these mechanisms first controlled and triggered by the fingers at that point migrated to the toes. Little by little, by moving down the leg, they gave birth to pedals that bear no resemblance to the big key of a low note: They are pedals that modify the *sound*, that stifle it, make it resonate, amplify it, color it [*timbrer*] in one way or another.

It is difficult to date the birth of these so-called *expression* pedals with any precision. This is all the more true given that various apparatuses long coexisted before definitively ending up in the feet. If the French-made keyboards seem to have been given knee-controlled mechanisms starting in the middle of the eighteenth century, there is much earlier evidence of the expressive use of the foot in England. In his 1676 *Musick's Monument*, Thomas Mace shows his enthusiasm for a "Late" and little-known "Invention" named "Pedal" because of its ability to produce "Varieties" of sound "with the Foot." "This Instrument," writes Mace with the childlike happiness of someone discovering a new corporeal pleasure, "is in Shape and Bulk, just like a Harpsicon"; it differs from it only through

> a kind of Cubbord, or Box, . . . which opens with a little Pair of Doors, in which Box the Performer sets both his

> Feet, resting them upon his Heels, (his Toes a little turning up) touching nothing, till such time as he has Pleasure to employ them . . . and so Causeth the whole Instrument to Sound, either Soft or Loud.

I like this naïve expression where, perhaps for the first time, we find the formulation of an unprecedented pleasure in playing, obtained *pedaliter* rather than *manualiter*. Mace truly seem to be *having a ball* [*prendre son pied*][3] with the four pedals activated in alternation (syntactically, the pleasure he speaks of can be tied to the use of the feet rather than to the pedals themselves).

Between these early testimonies and the first decades of the nineteenth century, the kneepads and pedals saw considerable development:[4] Not only did they activate muting pedals or apparatuses that raised the dampers (to allow the sound to resonate), but they also controlled mechanisms that produced variations in timbre in order to imitate the bassoon, the harp, as well as drums, cymbals, bells, and triangles (as a way of answering to the fashion for the "Turkish").

For this proliferation of pedals and effects, the 1833 journalist no longer has anything but scorn: "While one person thought they had found a pedal imitating the harps, someone else bragged that they had imitated the bassoon," he writes, adding that "the ridicule reached its peak through the drum, the bells, etc., etc." This is because, in the meantime, expression pedals will have been reduced and standardized as drastically as the fingering on the keyboard. In general, only two of these remain: forte or piano, damper or sustainer.

Nonetheless, beyond this reductive normalization, what remains is the *principle* of mobility and of a general transfer of the functions of the musician's body. The pedals—the feet—offer themselves as a substitute for certain roles previously assumed by the fingers, wrists, or forearms. The ligature [*liaison*] in particular. And it is sometimes said that they add a third hand ("In this way one can *figure* [*figurer*] three hands on the keyboard," writes our chronicler).

CHAPTER 12 *Joyful Tropiques (Evolution, Revolutions)*

Where then, exactly, might we say that rhetoric begins at the keyboard? Where does the proper end? Where do the figures and tropes emerge? Properly speaking, what is a hand-at-the-keyboard? And a foot? What is a proper-body-at-the-keyboard, and what are its organs?

In the history of keyboards, we cannot exactly say that the function creates the organ.

The organ-at-the-keyboard certainly does not preexist what it is summoned to play. The number of fingers is never set. Nor the number of hands, in fact. Everything depends on what one wants to tie or to untie [*lier ou délier*], and on how one goes about doing so.

Yet a stable function is not assigned to these organs, which are constantly being reborn. The keyboard is at best an open system of functional stand-ins [*suppléances*]: It is on the grounds of a defect that the infinite circulation of roles has always been set into motion and, hence, the whirling, the *tropology of the organs*. The theoreticians, rhetoricians, or didacticians all say so, each in turn.

Thus does François Couperin suggest that, at the keyboard, the way of releasing the note ("the cessation" and "the suspension of sounds") *takes the place* of the crescendo and diminuendo proper to bowed instruments:

> The sounds of the harpsichord have each been specifically determined and consequently cannot be increased or decreased. . . . In those places where the bowed instruments would increase their tone, the suspension at the harpsichord, by a contrary effect, seems to produce this desired result.[1]

Cessation and suspension are the substitutes for the bow against the backdrop of the keyboard's defects; they are its figures or its tropes by antiphrasis or ellipsis. (And in the same way, "in playing the organ or the harpsichord, the long mordent takes the place of the *martèlement* on bowed instruments" [35]: The trill is a *figure* for the violin's martellato.)

Carl Philipp Emanuel Bach, in turn, considers that at the keyboard there are indispensable ornaments: "The appoggiaturas are among the most necessary ornaments [*nöthigsten Manieren*]. They improve both the melody and the harmony. For the melody, they inspire something pleasant to the extent that they tie the notes together with one another [*indem sie die Noten gut zusammen hängen*]."[2]

The necessary ornaments—the paradoxical foundation of keyboard rhetoric—are not functional organs. They are substitutes, additions, "*agréments*," without which it would indeed not be possible to get by, but that remain infinitely replaceable in turn, on the basis of the keyboard's lack as described by Bach:

> Given that the long holding of the sound is lacking, in addition to its perfect decrease or increase—what in painting is called, not without reason, shadow and light—, it is no slight affair, on our instruments, to play an Adagio in a

singing way, without allowing too much spacing and uniformity because of the fact of an overly parsimonious padding [*ohne durch zu wenige Ausfüllungen zu viel Zeitraum und Einfalt blicken zu lassen*].[3]

The defects of the harpsichords, clavichords, or pianos, their discrete nature, the sonorous holes that are always threatening to open onto gaps and to damage the singing continuity of an adagio are the spring and axis for all of the turns—turns of the hand, turnings and tropes of organs—that are constantly recomposing the body-at-the-keyboard.

Chopin laconically gave the general syntax of this circulation of placeholders in a handwritten note for his unfinished method for piano: "*the wrist [:] the respiration in the voice*." This is a lapidary statement in which one could replace everything, except for the general form of equivalency: $x = y$ in z. With x for the foot, the forearm, the hand or the fingers; y for the *martellato* or the *legato*; z for the strings or the winds.

The list is open[4] in a whirlwind that draws me toward *a general organologics of the body as an infinite musical tropology.*

If anthropology studies the becoming of bodies on the scale of the evolution of the human species, if it follows their metamorphoses over the long haul, musical organology concerns itself with transformations, mutations, and transfers at a much faster tempo. It reveals an incredible cortege, a theory of mutants or monsters that follow one another at a frantic rhythm: They don't want anything to do with evolution; they only experience infinite revolutions.

It is this evolutionary short circuit that can be read in a precious document I found among the scattered papers of an old choirmaster by the name of Kreisler. He seems to have kept it in the hope of publishing it as an ironic allegory or fable of virtuoso pianists; but personally, I am not certain this is the best reading of this strange testimony.

Here it is; it's a "Letter from Milo, an educated ape, to his lady-friend Pipi in North America":

> You are aware, my sweet, that nature has endowed me with rather longish fingers; with these I can span fourteenths, even two octaves, and this, together with enormous skill in moving and animating my fingers, is my whole secret of fortepiano playing. My music-master shed tears of joy over the outstanding gifts of his pupil, for within a short time I reached the point where I could run up and down with both hands in demisemiquavers, hemidemisemiquavers, even semihemidemisemiquavers, without a mistake, play trills with all my fingers equally well, and execute leaps of three or four octaves up and down, just as I used to leap from one tree to the next. As a result I am the greatest virtuoso there can be. None of the available piano compositions is difficult enough for me, so I compose my sonatas and concertos myself. . . . I have also recently spoken to an instrument-maker about a fortepiano of nine to ten octaves. Can genius be limited to a meagre compass of seven wretched octaves? As well as the usual pedals for the Turkish drum and cymbal, he is to incorporate a trumpet pedal, and also a flageolet pedal to imitate as closely as possible the chirruping of birds. You see, dear Pipi, what sublime ideas a man of taste and education can conceive![5]

The letter is undated, and with good reason: This unequalled revolution of the organs—of the feet, hands, and fingers (of feet and hands)—is not localizable in a period or a phase of evolution; it happens every day, *effictively*, in sonorous body-to-body contacts.

CHAPTER 13 *Two Dispatches (One Fictive and the Other Dreamed Up)*

If the mutations of musicians' bodies ultimately take place very quickly in comparison to the more general laws of the evolution of the species, they often nonetheless take quite a while before it is possible to name, decipher, and read them. They can remain suspended for quite a while, in process, before benefiting from the powerful *effictions* that will take charge of them in order to construct other bodies in their image.

I recently discovered a dispatch that, though it came very quickly given that it was transported by the fastest means of telecommunication, has probably still not yet been deciphered. There are perhaps many people who read it before I did (it appeared in a German music journal in 1911); but because of the pseudonym with which its author thought he needed to sign it, it seems to me that it has never been taken seriously. It was dismissed as a joke. People thought they could forget it as just a good joke. Or a mere fiction. It's an April Fool's day trick, people imagined, with reference to its signature: *Aprilus Fischer*. (That the author was subsequently identified—as the pianist and composer Ferruccio Busoni—had no effect on the matter.)

This dispatch thus arrived too early. In other words, at bottom, it did not arrive at all: It did not find its addressee. It is still waiting to be read. Here it is, and I need to cite it almost in its totality:[1]

A Fairy-like Invention

New York, 1st April 1911

Wireless Despatch

[That we today, on 29th March, already know publicly what is only appointed to leave New York as a wireless dispatch on 1st April will seem less mysterious to the reader after he has finished reading this despatch. Compared with the discovery revealed here, this tiny anticipation of it seems a mere bagatelle.—Ed.]

An extraordinary discovery is announced from South Parkhill. Kennelton Humphrey Happenziegh, the scientist domiciled there—who is highly esteemed in professional circles but in no way celebrated—has succeeded, thanks to an unusual gift of sharp deduction, in arriving at far-reaching conclusions, through comparatively simple experiments. . . .

Happenziegh, of late, has been occupied with the preparation of a supersensitive apparatus (intended for phonographic disks). The contrivance, which he has perfected at last, resembles at a first glance a drum disk with a supersensitive epidermis, and possesses the quality of combining the utmost delicacy with the most complete power of resistance and is able to pick up noises which are inaudible or unintelligible to the human ear; moreover, it has the power of dissecting complicated sounds into their constituent parts. . . . The contrivance is so extremely delicate that when a hand is passed through hair the crackling is *distinctly* audible; light steps in the next room are recorded by it, the slightest breath is impressed on it. . . .

Happenziegh left his laboratory at two o'clock in the morning, after he had completed a new and (as he believed) perfect disk, and entered it again at six o'clock after a short night's rest.

He subjected his disk to an examination by means of a very powerful microscope constructed by him for this purpose, and discovered on it certain impressions which he could not account for. After he had separated the customary noises of the town at night, which he considered as secondary phenomena in this case, he found an accumulation of obscure diagrams which were systematic, complicated, and at first unintelligible. On first consideration they might have been of musical origin although they showed only a remote relationship with the musical forms familiar to him. In any case they must have come from a very great distance. An investigation as to whether within a ten-mile radius music might have been played that night and during those four hours, resulted in a negative answer. . . .

But the marks were imprinted and the disk, when it was brought into rotation, sounded music without doubt, which to the scholar's ears, however, remained as unintelligible as the diagrams had been to his eyes.

This happened about six months ago.

In between, Happenziegh had been at the work incessantly and his never-resting mind had succeeded in giving the solution to the riddle and in bringing forward a new theory, which fills us with awe and astonishment and opens up the widest prospects.

As the air needs an instrument to make its vibrations perceptible to our ear, so the air itself is only an instrument which transmits the not yet fully fathomed wavelengths. These original wavelengths, as Happenziegh recognizes, have the characteristic quality of being similarly effective in a time-sphere, as, for instance, wireless telegraphy in that of space.

In time its effect works as well backwards as forwards and its intensity decreases correspondingly with the distance.

Sound atmospherics, put in vibration through exterior impulse, continue in both directions. Its impressions will be passed on, into the past as well as into the future.

A scream fades away into tomorrow and the day after tomorrow and further, in corresponding strength—logically into yesterday and the day before yesterday also.

Thus, through a chance not yet cleared up, a demonstration of music in the future seems to have found its way on to the supersensitive disk and to have impressed itself there.

After laborious calculations (for which quite new estimations will have to be found) the origin of the phonographic marks might lie twenty to three hundred years in front of us (according to Happenziegh's assumption). If one takes an average figure, a hundred and forty years is the result, so that music written on the disk lies about a century and a half in the future. . . .

Sounds from the trombones like Aeolian harps melt into a sound fog, and again other voices out of the void, without audible beginning, disappear into the atmosphere of sound. Sounds as if coming from tinkling water and burning fire assume melodic form, appear and disappear.

Intervals are apparently purer and show the aliveness of human breath in their gradations and combinations.

Nature itself seems to sound, and we are tempted to suppose that this music never wearies and goes on creating from what is there into infinity.

All further details and additions to this sensational discovery we will communicate to our readers punctually and conscientiously every year.

Aprilus Fischer

That this dispatch was lost, immediately lost, is, at bottom, not in the least bit surprising. Because of its very structure, it could not arrive; it could not *take place*. There could not be an attributable place for what arrives (on March 29) before even leaving (on April 1), and which therefore perhaps never arrives.

Unlike its previous readers or nonreaders, I do not, however, think that this letter got lost in history's sorting merely as a consequence of the game Aprilus, its sender was playing with the postal service's stamps. Because if we look closely, this game has nothing gratuitous about it; it's anything but an April Fool's Day joke: The properly untimely nature of the letter—the apparent farce of its postal dressing—is in truth dictated by the very contents of the message.

What in effect does the dispatch say? It states and restates—it declares as a thesis and mimes as a narrative—this incredible affirmation (which is no doubt in a certain sense illegible): *Something is being written from the future.*

How are we to understand such a statement?

Quite simply, perhaps, by reading what is inscribed, by deciphering it. Not, however, by looking for a hidden allegorical or symbolic sense in the dispatch but by reading *literally* what is being written before our very eyes. Because even before saying anything else, the telegram simply states and restates this: Something was *written*, in other words engraved or inscribed, from the future, in a *medium*. Yet what is inscribed somewhere perhaps always comes from the future and not, as we so often imagine, from an archived past: that the source shone from yesterday or from tomorrow, it remains that it remains to be read. And reread. In this sense, it remains yet to come: *post(e)-restante*.

The telegram received from Aprilus Fischer is *wireless*: without a tie, a pure interruption in the course of time, a pure event, which therefore in a certain way does not (yet) arrive. Such are also the signs left on the membrane, on the disk.[2] The event of the telegram is the echo of the equally interruptive or eruptive one of the signs that have occurred.

Let us therefore look more closely, I say to myself, at the "medium," that is to say the infra-thin skin that was able to provoke such a "miracle," in the words of the editor.

Indeed, the membrane of Happenziegh's disk is not a membrane like the others. It indeed looks like a drum's skin, or a tympanum, but it has a property that no drum or tympanum has probably ever had: It keeps and archives what strikes it before *rendering* it. It therefore works in both directions: It receives and it renders. Gift for gift, something loaned for something rendered.

Without this membrane that is in a way reversible, without this infra-thin medium that has nonetheless already been shared in its thickness between reception and retransmission, all the symmetries or inversions mentioned by Aprilus could not take place in the narrative. It is therefore on the basis of this kind of *tain* of the phonic mirror that all the effects of the image's reversal emerge: symmetries between past and future, between space and time, the arrival before departure.

One of the most remarkable inversions in Aprilus's narrative concerns air: "As the air needs an instrument to make its vibrations perceptible to our ear, so the air itself is only an instrument which transmits the not yet fully fathomed wavelengths," writes the wireless telegraphist. Yet good sense and the right direction [*le bon sens et dans le bon sens*] would lead us to think that it is the instrument (of music) that needs air to transmit its vibrations; whereas here, on the contrary, it is the air that looks like [*l'air qui a l'air*] it is playing, and the instrument transmits.

We should, however, not conclude from this that music (this particular piece or any other that ended up being inscribed) is "timeless": eternally straddling the aerial waves waiting to be incarnated here or there, when one is willing to catch it in order to give it an instrumental and resonating body. It is rather that, as soon as it has gained access to presence through the medium that welcomes it, it *immediately* sees itself detached and dismissed from any identifiable date. It is as if it took place without taking place, precisely. What makes it happen is also what, from the start, takes it away or displaces it: Happenziegh's infra-thin phonographic membrane digs out or divides the punctual source it captures; and this source then stretches and empties out, radically disjoins itself from all origins and from all full presence to distend between future and past.

The fable's membrane is not a musical instrument some interpreter is playing; it's a skin that allows itself to be touched by invisible forces. This resonator that seems to start resounding *on its own* could, at this point, be called *autophonic*. A kind of *automembranophone* that does not have a musician, just as the dispatch has no addressee.

As such, the thin layer is related to a whole family, to a whole paradigm of autophonic instruments that predated the phonograph and were often associated with the supernatural. This is the case in an exemplary way of the Aeolian harp, about which Novalis wrote:

> Subjects and objects must exist at once, like the sounds of the Aeolian harp, without cause—without betraying their instrument.[3]

One could not find a better way to describe the occurrence that Aprilus is also talking about.

"Nature is an Aeolian harp," says another of Novalis's fragments. So much so that the irruptive and unassignable nature of the sounds it produces, along with its identification with nature itself, perhaps make of this instrument, and despite their clear morphological differences, the veritable precursor of Happenzeigh's skin. Aprilus's dispatch actually says this explicitly: The sounds restituted by the membrane are "like Aeolian harps," and it is "*Nature itself* [that] seems to sound."

In the West, musical instruments have long been classified into three types: strings, winds, percussions. And from this classificatory point of view, it seems strange to say that a membranophone struck like the quasi drum in the dispatch was able to be preceded or prefigured by a cordophone like the Aeolian harp. It is perhaps not any more surprising than so many of the other things Aprilus recounts, but this does not provide easy satisfaction for our rationality.

To this objection, I will briefly respond here by referring to authors who were capable of recognizing the fact that the classifications of musical instruments were only ever *relative*. This is notably the case of Marin Mersenne, who writes in his 1636 *Harmonie universelle*:

> All bodies that make noise and render a perceptible sound when they are struck, can be placed in the class of Percussion instruments, and consequently the string instruments can be described in this book, since they are struck with the finger, the palm, or otherwise.[4]

Mersenne goes on to concede that the "beating" of the strings "is so light that it should be called a simple touch, or a simple traction, rather than a beating, or a percussion." And this is why he, too, will leave it up to usage, to the habit that makes it so that, among the instruments, "we ordinarily distinguish the ones we hit with a hammer or a stick from those that are touched differently." But in the end, he seems to say, if we put ourselves in the more general perspective of a *history of the touching of bodies*, the usual classification would not necessarily be the most interesting one. In any case, the Aeolian harp is not in and of itself incompatible with a struck surface, especially if both this one and that one are in fact brushed without there truly being any percussion.

In addition, before finally dissolving his treatise into the inherited and established categories, Mersenne will have suggested an entirely different classification, one that is at the very least surprising and that interests me because of what it seems to capture from Aprilus's message in advance. "We can divide all the instruments into immobile and mobile ones," Mersenne in effect writes.[5] An unprecedented division that he explains and exemplifies in the following way: "The mobile ones include all those that use strings, and pipes, bells, and generally everything that perceptibly moves, either through the mere fluttering of the air, or in any other way one wants." The immobile ones, in contrast,

> belong to bodies that are so struck by the winds, or the waves, that they make no perceptible movement, like rocks and mountains: because though several argue they tremble, and that sound cannot be made without the trembling of bodies . . . , this trembling is nonetheless not perceived, and it seems that the tremblings and flutterings of the air that hits the rocks, and other similar bodies, are enough to engender the sounds we hear.

For Mersenne, the "noises of the wind and thunder," because they "do not depend on our will," are a part of this category that, to my knowledge, he is the first to propose. I find myself dreaming of a forgotten dispatch from Mersenne, where he would speak of Aeolian harps or, who knows, of skins that are immobile but struck by the winds that transport the air charged with sounds.

Many of the phenomena at work in the body-to-body contact of Monk or the Nephew would certainly find themselves enlightened by it.

CHAPTER 14 Organologics (2): Autophony

Autophony, yes, is no doubt the most idio(ma)tic musicality there is. That is, the most proper, the most specific to sound-producing instruments and bodies *as such*.

Blacksmiths that strike without understanding or hearing anything; a Nephew that, as a phonographic membrane, allows himself to vibrate according to the waves that hit it; Monk dazed in front of his mechanical piano as it plays all by itself; a monkey—Milo—going up and down the keyboard at random—all of these are figures that a respectable and reasonable organology has a duty to dismiss as jokes or bad dreams. As monsters of fiction, chimera like Glenn Steinway.

And yet this omnipresent autophony that haunts the corpus is constantly reemerging. It is the one dictating its law to organic logic, to the organologic registering the evolution of sound-producing bodies.

Autophony is as old as the world.

The Chinese, says André Schaeffner in his major treatise on modern organology,[1] put "little whistles made from fine gourds called *ko-tzé* onto the tails of pigeons." The traveling birds then became the carriers "of a ravishing Aeolian harp, as light as a soap bubble and admirably sculpted." There are also "whistles, flutes or Aeolian reeds" that find themselves "fixed onto the backs of kites."

From Greco-Roman antiquity, thanks in particular to Vitruvius, we are today still aware of the hydraulic organ, whose invention is attributed to Ctesibius; we also know many other machines "of different kinds, that allow us to see that, by compressing liquids through the means of the air, one produces effects similar to nature's." These "organs that play by means of water" imitate "the song of blackbirds" and "allow other pleasant sounds to be heard."[2]

All of these Aeolian apparatuses, whether moved by climatic, mechanical, hydraulic, or animal forces, give voice to a kind of second nature, like the immobile bodies "hit by the winds" in Mersenne's classification. Yet if Western organology long considered these instruments mere curiosities, this is ultimately perhaps because it could not or did not want to see the law, in truth the only available *model*, to think its own project: a filiation of sound-producing bodies *among themselves*, their origins in which the so-called "human" body ("my" body) would only be a particular, if certainly remarkable, case. It is thus perhaps that, in the end, and despite all the instrumental idioms that it ended up including, organology was unable to take the decision to break with the anthropocentric logic of the evolution of bodies.[3]

It is true that it is not easy to include the idea of an unlimited factory of *organa* spouting from a melting pot of gathered musical idiotisms. It is understandable that reason refuses and resists, that it does not want to untie the bond that ties a reasonable (rather than a resonant) human body to bodies that must remain *its* instruments. And its *instruments*, in other words its tools for its musical service. Can we go beyond such a resistance to open the thinking of sound bodies to their reciprocal plasticity? Can we *seriously* make an argument capable of welcoming hands with more than ten fingers, feet that breathe like lungs, and harpsichords that give birth?

Everywhere, the organological corpus bears the traces or symptoms of its resistance.

Starting with the very history of the word *autophone.*

To my knowledge, Athanasius Kircher is the first, in his 1650 *Musurgia universalis*, to have used the term to designate an apparatus that mechanically produces music *on its own.* But at the end of the nineteenth century, Victor-Charles Mahillon gives it another meaning that, with a few adjustments, will prevail in modern organology: In 1880, in his *Catalogue du musée instrumental de Bruxelles*, he defines it as follows (emphasis mine): "We call *autophones* those instruments made of solid bodies, elastic enough *on their own* to sustain the vibratory movement that is provoked in them through one of the three following ways of starting: percussion, pinching, or rubbing." One sees the slide: Autophones are no longer endowed with their own *activity*; they merely have a physical property that—as it is particularly the case of bells or other metallophones—allows them to vibrate for a long time without its being necessary to stretch them out initially, unlike drums and other membranophones, for example. Mahillon seems to not have been aware of the term used by Kircher. And it is only a bit later that another organologist, Curt Sachs, realized the ambiguity attached to the name (if not to the objects) of the category thus constituted. In 1913, in his *Reallexikon der Musikinstrumente*, he wrote:

> Mahillon has the great merit of having grouped together into one category, under the name of autophonous instruments, all the sound tools that are resonant *according to their nature*, in other words whose substance is itself elastic enough to be set into vibration by being struck, pinched,

> rubbed, perhaps even with breath; unlike those whose vibrating substance must first be *artificially stretched*, like membrane or string instruments. . . . The organological system will always have to count with the class whose boundaries are defined in this way, but it will not be able to keep its name because the nonspecialist will understand that it is an instrument playing by itself, an automatic instrument. We therefore suggest the appellation "idiophone" for this class, in other words instruments "resonant according to their nature."[4]

What these lexicographical manipulations reveal is indeed organology's resistance to welcoming autophony as a fully recognized category. In the classification proposed the following year, in 1914, by Curt Sachs and Erich von Hornbostel[5]—a founding classification that is still in use today—the criteria of automation will actually be mentioned only very late in the game, after the instruments have already been distributed according to the trunks, branches, and reeds of this arborescent cartography of sound-producing bodies. It intervenes at the end of the race, like an optional suffix that one can add or not to the numbered nomenclature that gives every instrument its place, in a classification inspired by librarians. This is what in fact explains that the phonograph simply has no existence for these authors. The instrument that serves as the basis for the investigations of the ethnomusicologists that Sachs and Hornbostel *also* are, the instrument that allows all the instruments of the world to speak *on their own*, is notable for its absence.

Mersenne and several others had nonetheless allowed it to be understood that autophony could very well be the *very first characteristic* for distinguishing certain sonorous bodies. André Schaeffner will state this once again, in his way, in the critique he makes of Sachs: "Some Aeolian mouth harp or *sanza* left to its own, set to work through a breath that nothing governs . . . would be that instrument of Utopia that neither Mahillon nor Professor Sachs has glimpsed in creating the terms *autophone* and *idiophone*."[6] If this critique could not be more legitimate, one must nonetheless go even further to say that the original autophony has nothing utopian about it. Far from being from nowhere, it actually spreads out *everywhere*.

It is on this basis that we may start to think that the idiotisms of sonorous bodies generate *organa* among themselves that are as improbable as the supernumerary members that abound in the history of music. For what tool, attached to its anthropic raison d'être, would ever have dared give birth to more than two hands or to more than ten fingers? What instrument in the service of an all too human music would ever have opened the door to the *entropy* of bodies? To the chance of their occasions?

CHAPTER 15 Genesis (1): Ocular Harpsichord, Organ of Flavors

In the dream that d'Alembert has, it is in the middle of the bits of sentences and disjointed words that a proper name emerges, or rather floats; through it, one of the most surprising construction sites of resonant bodies transits. D'Alembert is delirious, and in his trance of possession a strange figure returns, that of a fabulous *maker of bodies* [*facteur de corps*]: Castel, the father Castel, whose name slips into the middle of the dreamer's murmurings.

Of what is Castel the trace? What huge chain of *effictions* rushes into his name to shine all over in Diderot's corpus?

Castel: harpsichord.

The figure of the harpsichord literally haunts Diderot's writings, far beyond the harpsichord-body that is whispered to d'Alembert. It sometimes takes on the figure of an *ocular harpsichord*,[1] whose inventor is the father Castel, a Jesuit, and to whom an article of the *Encyclopedia* is devoted, at the letter C, as is fitting.[2] In order to understand what the stakes offered by this instrument are, we might as well read the minute description Diderot gives of it here:

> OCULAR HARPSICORD (*Mus. and Opt.*), keyboard instrument analogous to the auricular harpsichord composed of

as many colored octaves as the auricular harpsichord's sonorous octaves organized in tones and half-tones, destined to give to the soul through the eyes the same pleasant sensations of melodies and harmonies of colors as those of the melodies and harmonies of sounds that the ordinary harpsichord communicates to it through the ear.

What must one have to make an ordinary harpsichord? Strings tuned according to a certain system of music, and the means to make these strings resonate. What must one have for an *ocular harpsichord*? Colors tuned according to the same system as the sounds, and the way of producing them for the eyes: but one is as possible as the other is. . . .

What is playing? For the ordinary harpsichord, it is sounding and staying quiet, or appearing and disappearing to the ear. What will playing be for the *ocular harpsichord*? Showing oneself and keeping oneself hidden, or appearing and disappearing to the eye: And since auricular music has twenty or thirty ways of producing sounds, through strings, pipes, voices, violins, basses, lyres, guitars, fifes, flageolets, bassoons, serpents, trumpets, organs, etc., ocular music will have as many corresponding ways of producing the colors, boxes, fans, suns, stars, paintings, natural and artificial lights, etc. That is how it is done. . . .

One can imagine such a machine without being well versed in music and in optics; one can execute it with success without being a rare machinist. The famous F. Castel Jesuit is its inventor; he announced it in 1725. The construction of this instrument is so extraordinary that it is only the meagerly enlightened public that can complain that it is always being made and that it is never completed.

Extraordinary instrument, in effect, that claims to construct in the workshop of its maker a new organ, an eye-ear [*oeil-oreille*], a monstrous *eyear* [*oroeil*] that would bring together in an unprecedented and unheard-of way the fibers or strings of two senses that until then were distinct. The ocular harpsichord, if its construction had been able to be completed one day, would have been the experience answering to the *effiction* of the *Conversation with d'Alembert* according to which "our senses are as many keys" on that "organized keyboard" that we are.

Before fascinating Diderot and some of his contemporaries,[3] this uncompleted harpsichord—as we are—this ocular harpsichord had no less *effictive* antecedents it is important to remember here.

Castel explicitly recognized his debt to another Jesuit who preceded him: Athanasius Kircher, the inventor of the category of autophones. Castel pays him a vibrant homage in a posthumous text:

> Since the beginning of time, light has been compared with sound; but I know of no one who pushed this parallel further than Kircher. . . . Now Kircher does not hesitate to call sound the ape of light, and bravely advances the idea, not without having thoroughly thought it through, that everything that makes itself perceptible to the eyes can be made perceptible to the ear, and reciprocally that everything that is the object of hearing can become the object of sight. One must note, first, that sound spreads all around, as light does, in straight lines; second, that when it encounters impenetrable bodies, it is reflected and reflects itself, third, in equal angles, like light; fourth, that if the bodies are penetrable, it penetrates them, by suffering, as light does, a refraction that turns it a bit away from its path . . . ; fifth, the light meeting a concave body is reflected at a point where its reunion forms an ardent foyer: Sound, when it encounters concave bodies, is reflected at a point where its

reunion also forms a resonant foyer, in other words an echo.[4]

But Castel does not stop with crediting Kircher for having systematized these analogies between the two senses. He makes of him a veritable *manufacturer of organs* so true is it that by equipping hearing or sight with prostheses, one reinvents them, one turns them into unprecedented keys on the keyboard of the senses; Castel continues:

> One makes far-seeing glasses that make distant objects present to the eyes: Did Kircher not teach us to make far-hearing glasses, in other words speaking trumpets? . . . I will push the comparison all the way through, even though anti-analogists should be enraged by it. One makes microscopes to distinguish the smallest objects: Will you really believe that one makes microscopes for the ear as a way of distinguishing the smallest and most inarticulate sounds? And does one not, & does Kircher not teach how to make the horns that a deaf person puts to his ear in order to gather the least powerful sounds? . . . Why, I was saying, by following this analogy's thread, why would one not make ocular harpsichords, just as we make auricular ones? It is once again to Kircher that I owe the birth of such a joyful idea.

Contemporary with Castel's harpsichord, other keyboards were imagined, for other weavings among the senses. There is, for example, the organ of tastes a certain Polycarpe Poncelet describes in his *Chemistry of Taste and Smell* published in Paris in 1755. "Flavors," we read in it, "consist in more or less strong vibrations of salts that act on the sense of taste, as sounds consist in the more or less strong vibrations of the air that acts on the sense of hearing," so much so that there may be "a Music for the tongue & the palate, as there is one for the ears."[5] The author legitimates the audacity of his project by referring to the precedent and model furnished by the ocular harpsichord:

> Among the singular productions from a playful imagination, the famous ocular harpsichord deserves a distinguished place: its success was probably not impossible, since there are seven primitive colors that, like the sounds and flavors, can be infinitely combined in a harmonic progression & consequently provide the basis for an ocular Music.

The flavorful keyboard will therefore be "like a new genre of Organ, on which one will be able to play all sorts of Airs." And thinking of those who could not or wouldn't want to practice playing this new instrument, Polycarpe Poncelet provides for veritable *flavorful autophones* on mechanical cylinders on which the gustative melodies will be inscribed: "One will be able to construct sorts of small barrel organs [*turlutaines*], comparable to *serinettes*, thanks to which [these people] will painlessly play . . . 10, 20, 30 airs, more or less, according to whether the cylinder is more or less charged." The keyboard equipment little by little touches all the senses, as Castel himself had imagined, he who, in addition to his "Harpsichord for the eyes" described its generalization in a "Harpsichord for the Senses":

> Place around forty pots full of diverse perfumes. Cover them with valves, & make it so that the movement of the keys opens the valves: that's for the nose. On a plank, arrange in a certain distribution bodies capable of making different impressions on the hand, & then pass it evenly over these bodies: that's for touch. Arrange in the same

way bodies agreeable to taste, mixed in with some bitterness.[6]

In all these uncompleted attempts, both fabulous and fabulating, we can glimpse the powerful fictional efficacy of a *general organology of the senses*: a veritable treatise of instrumentation and manufacture of what will later be called synesthesia.[7]

In order to find something like the matrix of these joyful assemblages, one has to return to Kircher himself, to his theological fable that turns God into an organist and Genesis into an affair of keyboards and register.

Here we can read from his *Musurgia universalis* published in Rome in 1650:

> Let us now show how, in this first origin of things, the organist, Creator of all things, God played.
>
> The Craftsman [*Opifex*] who has the intention of constructing an Organ has thus first posed different substructures, as one poses the first elements of a work, then made pipes of all kinds, disposed the air pipes and wind conductors, and for the demonstration of a greater diversity of harmonies, adopted diverse rules [*canones*] that are commonly called Registers; he then orders the bellows, those reserves of wind from which the air, in perpetual movement, compressed and constrained into the conduits, is sufficiently furnished; to conclude, he places the Keyboard [*Claviarium*], this ultimate director of his practical knowledge, and finally, through the work of the fingers and the varied combination of registers, touching the strip of wood or *palmulas* that we call keys [*tastos*], he produces that variety of harmony that we feel with admiration in organs. It is no differently that God, Great and Perfect, in order to

> fabricate the dissonant-consonant organ of the world in its inexhaustible variety, first assembled, through the power of his Word, that matter without form and that chaos without order which became so to speak the substructures and preliminaries [*praeludia*] of the future organ; then, for the pipes, he drew out certain rudiments of latent forms in this formless chaos; third, . . . by incubating them he engendered the formless waters and the air and the winds necessary for the breath of the future organ; fourth, . . . he disposed this formless mass of materials imbued with various and different sounds into the separate classes of things, in other words into certain registers; fifth, he produced the Keyboard of the whole organ which is its soul and its Art. . . . With the work finally finished, this supreme Archimusician, setting the organ's keyboard into motion with the breath of his spirit, that is with his art, produced that admirable harmony of things that we still admire today.
>
> . . . soon there emerged, through consonance and dissonance, something like a gathering and a concert, a symphony [*contextus concentusque & symphonia*] such that, right up to today, we hear this spectacle through the eyes with admiration and we look at it through our ears with astonishment.[8]

Yes, you read that right: we *hear through our eyes* and we *look through our ears . . .* [*oculis audimus, & auribus spectamus*]. The Great Organist will have been the first to open up the possibility of recomposing the connections of the senses with which he endowed us.

The question that remains for us who come after so many fabulous manufacturers is the following: How can we think of this incessantly revived manufacture of feeling bodies outside all explicit—or implicit and underground—reference to the powerful image of divine endowment? How, after having thought we had broken with the pious rationality of the musicus dear to the Christian Middle Ages, do we avoid giving ourselves over body and soul to what Schoenberg religiously called "the programme of the Creator who, on the great rationing day, allotted us so and so many arms, legs, ears and other organs"?[9]

CHAPTER 16 *Telepathy*

In *D'Alembert's Dream*, right in the middle of her debate with Doctor Bordeu, at the bedside of the one who is sleeping and delirious, Mademoiselle de l'Espinasse happens upon a question that, she says, "I should have thought about earlier": "Why, in fact, don't I think throughout my body?"[1]

Bordeu answers her dogmatically: "It's because consciousness has only one location." His interlocutrice, who finds the answer a bit short and tidy, is perplexed ("Well, there's a quick answer").

I will not, however, affirm that he is wrong, nor that the polylogue orchestrated by Diderot shows that he is simply wrong or right. I would have simply been happy, leaving consciousness there where it can be found, to have interfered in this scene, in this curious *remue-ménage à trois*, to ask Bordeu the question of the *transmission of thought*. Because Mademoiselle de l'Espinasse was indeed asking about thought, not about consciousness.

It may well be that only God spreads his consciousness everywhere. His omniconsciousness. But what about thought? And what about *musical* thought?

Among all questions this one is particularly important to me, for, faced with the dissemination and *composition* of bodies that I am trying to have us understand, a stubborn and insistent objection is advanced, which says:

"OK, so you argue that *there are* bodies that compose themselves among one another. OK, so you don't want to secure them to that center that man (or God) was. But in this pure *partes extra partes*, in this simple co-presence or co-resonance of extended bodies from whose perspective you like to contemplate the emergence of lawless *organa*, how do you explain that there are tendencies, directions, recurrences, and persistences? How do you manage to avoid quite simply leaving it up to the poor observation of the chaos of worlds?"

"Damn! I don't know. I'm not sure I'm not giving voice to chaos, in effect. You are going to laugh (and perhaps there is in fact nothing to be done but to laugh about it, or to play on it): I believe, as a matter of fact, in a form of telepathy."

"So *that* is your answer?"

"It is one possible answer; allow me to argue it for a bit."

Try for one moment to lend an ear, seriously, to the testimony of Marie Jaëll, who was an extraordinary pianist.[2] Try, as I am trying to do, not to occult too quickly what she says, try not to scornfully dismiss her argument, which is effectively colored by the obscurest occultisms. Listen to her:

> Space is sonorous [she writes]. I feel my fingers moving in this sonorous space. It is changed when my fingers run through it. Space is attractive. The fingers are attracted when they move. . . . It's the discovery of musical magnetism through the hand, which rises before me.[3]

Here, her hand is erected as a body. Elsewhere, she relates how, faced with trees that "raise their fat leafless branches," she was "struck to see the gigantic mental image of [her] two hands suddenly appear." But this image is more than an image: It's an *effiction* that fabricates, shapes, or fictions a new body for her. And it is once she is endowed with these new organs that, for example, she will go listen to Liszt, that she will hear him play like no one else: "When, in 1868, in Rome, I heard Liszt for the first time, all of my auditory faculties seemed to be transformed as soon as he started to play," she writes, before giving voice to her singular *audiovision* of the virtuoso's fingers and hands:

> Thanks to this quadruple mirror with which each of his fingers must have been equipped, Liszt's hand looked nothing like ours, because we do not feel the activity of a single finger reflecting the lively strength of the other fingers. In reality, we do not know that if in each hand the pianist plays with only five fingers, his brain should operate as if it were perceiving twenty-five of them in each hand.[4]

Here it's thinking everywhere, in all the fingers. And *between the fingers*. The reference to the brain as center should not deceive us: It is indeed *in every finger* that, for Marie Jaëll, all the others are present to one another.

But you will say to me that this is only a way of extending the "conscious" center, of diffusing it in an occult way through the body, without in any way harming the logic of a soul governing the members.

It's truc. I'll give you that.

Which is why I must appeal to another witness, one less suspect of occultism: Freud.

Freud, in some of his writing, and not without a certain uneasiness, broached the subject of the strange analogies between dreams and radiotelegraphic radiation. Thus in the second of his *New Introductory Lectures on Psycho-Analysis*, titled "Dreams and Occultism," Freud, after having recalled the usual sense of the word *telepathy* ("an event which occurs

. . . at about the same moment to the consciousness of someone distant in space, without the paths of communication that are familiar to us coming into question"), Freud, then, gives the following example:

> Person A may be the victim of an accident or may die, and Person B, someone nearly attached to him—his mother or daughter or fiancée—learns the fact at about the same time through a visual or auditory perception. In this latter case, then, it is *as if she had been informed by telephone*, though such was not the case; it is a kind of psychical counterpart to *wireless telegraphy*.[5]

This analogy between a psychic phenomenon and a material apparatus (the telephone, then radiotelegraphy) is then abandoned, and Freud pursues the presentation of different cases and examples—"as though," he says, "I believed in the objective reality of the phenomenon of telepathy." It is only at the end of the lecture that the analogy reemerges:

> The telepathic process is supposed to consist in a mental act in one person instigating the same mental act in another person. What lies between these two mental acts may easily be a physical process into which the mental one is transformed at one end and which is transformed back once more into the same mental one at another end. The analogy with other transformations, such as occur in speaking and hearing by telephone, would then be unmistakable. And only think if one could get hold of this physical equivalent of the psychical act![6]

Beyond the different cases presented, beyond Freud's (feigned or real) indecision about his own opinion,[7] the fact remains that the *telephonopathic* analogy haunts this lecture.

From the telephone to wireless telegraphy, the discourse on telepathy or telesthesia[8] is molded in the lexicon of the apparatuses of sound transmission and reproduction (it is in this sense that Freud speaks of a "physical process").

"OK," you say to me, "let's admit that psychic processes can be translated, or 'transposed,' as Freud writes, into physical apparatuses. But how does this hypothesis give you access to a composition of bodies among themselves? Is it not, on the contrary, a way of *diffusing* the soul (the psyche) through bodies, and thus of endowing that center with which you seek to break the ties with a ubiquity that only further ensures them?"

"Perhaps," indeed. But allow me to take things one step further in our debate. Allow me one last ante, one last bet. Listen now to Walter Benjamin when, in a posthumous note, he analyzes *gambling*. Yes, gambling and the gambler, someone who plays not music, but roulette, not in a concert hall or a chamber, then, but at a casino:

> A game room is an exceptional laboratory for telepathic experiments. One must first admit that a lucky gambler is in telepathic contact, and then that this contact is established between him and the ball, not between him and the dealer who puts it in motion. For if the contact were established with the dealer, the gambler's task would be not to allow this contact to be troubled by anyone else. Now if we think of the violence and passion with which, in a game room, desire, the need to be given support, and curiosity can turn gamblers toward one another, we can measure just how difficult it is to turn these attentions away from oneself and thus remove oneself from any hostile suggestion. This attitude of the gambler, both tense and internally supple, cannot be conquered from within through *obsti-*

> *nacy* [*entêtement*], to which the losing gambler takes frequent recourse to succeed only in losing even more.[9]

The telepathy in question, as we see, is not *first of all* a relation from soul to soul, between the gambler and the dealer; it is initiated between the gambler and the ball. And it does not go through the "head" [*tête*], through the effusion of an obstinate [*entêtée*] will or intention (Benjamin writes the word in French), but through the fingers and hands. In another fragment devoted to gambling,[10] Benjamin in fact specifies that it is "motor innervation" that is "decisive," since the gambler has to make his hands "responsive to the slightest innervations." "The gambler's basic approach," he adds, is felt "at the last moment, when everything is pressing toward a conclusion, at the critical moment of danger": Then his ability "of reading the table at a glance—*if this, too, is not just an expression from the realm of optics*—" properly erupts (emphasis mine): Here it is indeed a matter of *reading at a distance through the fingers*, not through the eyes.

Now this reading with one's fingertips, so similar to that of so many keyboardists (especially once they, like Monk, devote themselves to *improvisation*), is never a gift or a given. As Benjamin writes:

> Also established is the fact that no one has so many chances of betting on a winning number as someone who has just made a significant win. This means that the correct sequence is based not on any previous knowledge of the future but on a correct physical predisposition, which is increased in immediacy, certainty, and uninhibitedness *by every confirmation, such as is provided by a win.*[11]

Fragility of the innervation, then, is not distributed or won in advance but is strengthened by the very road it clears through its repeated opportunities: It maintains itself with the chance that, at every instant, can also annihilate it as if it had never existed. Which is to say that in playing (and of course, for my part, I am talking about musical play), the vibrating fibering of bodies is constructed without foundations, grows its roots and branches in the improvised air of its occasions.

And yet no doubt unlike the games of chance on the basis of which I seek to understand them, musical bodies, which we believe to be aerial and hollow and resonant like dreams, leave lasting traces of their effictive effusions; they are embodied in archives, prostheses, maculatures, instruments, *organa*.

CHAPTER 17 Scruples (Clones and Stand-ins)

The scrupulous part of me would like to drive my point home. And find, against the objector, a firm and definitive response to the doubt he formulates in the following way: "But do you really think it is enough to take everything literally, word by word? Is it really enough to imagine 'effictively' (as you say, not without camouflaging the problem) twenty-five fingers, three hands, toes that breathe, and so on, in order to confer a *tangible* existence for them? And supposing we even go that far, that we play your game, do we not, precisely, run the risk of making all the musical bodies a merely imaginative game, a mere fable? Thus of placing their corporeality even more radically under erasure than by limiting ourselves to the anthropological reasoning that counts only ten fingers, two hands, and so on?"

Before leaving these objections to their obstinate insistence, the scrupulous one in me would like to add a few words.

"Music," I will say, "by giving body to unprecedented *organa* and by delivering them to lasting *effictions*, *short-circuits* physiological evolution and its reason(s). Not only by placing it in between parentheses, by *suspending* it, but also, and above all, by *accelerating* it. It can be seen as a kind of momentary accelerator of the incubation of bodies and members of all kinds. Because of this, it can be said to anticipate future possibilities; it would be the gamble on the fact that, one day, yes, bodies, *in effect(s), will become*."

It is in laughing, and playing, too, that the interlocutors of the *Interview* and the *Dream* imagine the becoming of bodies, including their cloning and their hybridizations before the fact, beyond good and evil. Thus, in this fragment noted by Mademoiselle de l'Espinasse, where d'Alembert glimpses in a dream "a human society . . . and an entire region populated by the fragment of a single individual," "human polyps": "all that is very pleasant to imagine," he says, before he cracks into "bursts of laughter."[1] The organological fiction reaches its peak here at the Sabbath or ballet of bodies: "So it could be that the Cyclops was not a creature out of fables"; "the animal will have . . . three feet, four arms, or six fingers on each hand" (189). "What do you think of mixing the species?" In short, according to Bordeu, who is relating what the dreamer says, "Nothing that exists can be either against nature or outside of nature" (230). It's just that, in nature and according to nature, it takes time. Because, as d'Alembert says in another dream fragment noted by Mademoiselle de l'Espinasse, "Perhaps, in order to renew species it requires ten times longer than the period assigned for their duration" (176).

It is much more quickly, and *provisionally*, that music, without morals, without laughter or tears, but certainly while playing, metamorphoses the *organa* and like a lie or a ruse provisionally transfigures the body, for example, by making it blush, before it returns to its habitual carnation.[2]

And what if it didn't return to it?

The fleeting trace through which music inscribes in various bodies the mark of a new fabrication is bound to survive; it is bound to return, carried as it is by the *carrier waves*—as one could say, using a radiophonic lexicon—of resonators and modulated as it is by the modulating waves of fictions. Music would thus generalize, beyond all experimental psychology, the experience of *phantom limbs*.

To d'Alembert, who asks him, "Given all the vicissitudes which I've been through in the course of my life . . . how have I retained my identity for other people and for myself?" Bordeu answers in substance, "because of the slowness of the changes." In effect, "If you'd passed in the wink of an eye from youth to decrepitude, you'd been thrown into this world as if at the first moment of your birth, and you'd not have been yourself either to others or to yourself."

This *if*, this conditional that prudently restrains the consequence that Bordeu draws from it, sees itself raised into music, so to speak; the transport through the ages would be *the very condition* of the evolutions of the sound-producing bodies at work. This is why music, the lightning-flash bricolage of musical organology would have a close tie to childhood, as the birth that is prolonged after birth.

Speaking of the childhood experience of the body, Benjamin writes:

> For the child, it is just as obvious to walk backward as forward. Moving forward imposes itself only after a process of selection. When the child pulls a horse behind him, it is therefore on the one hand an expression of his indifference to the categories of front and behind. On the other hand, we should perhaps look for something like a stand-in of its own back—something like a living and autonomous back.[3]

This childhood "joy" Benjamin is speaking of, that joy into which music throws bodies by plunging them back beyond the slow "selection process," this pleasure in playing not only would accompany the body's escape from itself (the back living its own life), but it would also sketch out the possibility, for what escapes this way, of deposing itself and crystallizing in autonomous "stand-in" *organa:* the horse, over there, at the end of a string, like a back dispatched and on the verge of being detached.

CHAPTER 18 **Conducting (Seen from the Back)**

"The joy of pulling a little horse: of driving a train," Walter Benjamin also says in the same fragment on the child. "Being followed on one's own path. Making noise behind oneself."[1]

I know of at least one musical body whose experience comes close, in a strangely familiar and sometimes uncanny way, to that of the child pulling her train behind herself, from the back.

It's that of the orchestra conductor.

The orchestra conductor, yes, with his properly magical power for animating bodies, as Elias Canetti described him in an unforgettable scene:

> In front of him sits the orchestra and behind him the audience. He stands on a dais and can be seen both from in front and from behind. In front his movements act on the orchestra and behind on the audience. . . . Quite small movements are all he needs to wake this or that instrument to life or to silence it at will. He has the power of life and death over the voices of the instruments; one long silent will speak again at his command. . . . During a concert, and for the people gathered together in the hall, the conductor

is a leader. He stands at their head *with his back to them. It is him they follow*, for it is he who goes first. But, instead of his feet, it is his hands which lead them. The movement of the music, which his hands bring about, represents the path his feet would be the first to tread. The crowd in the hall is carried forward by him. During the whole performance of a work they never see his face. He is merciless: there are no intervals for rest. *They see his back always in front of them*, as though it were their goal. If he turned round even once the spell would be broken. The road they were travelling would suddenly cease to exist and there would be nothing but a hall full of disillusioned people without movement or impetus.[2]

The orchestra conductor *conducts*, as the English language says—and in French, Berlioz, in his 1855 work, still uses the word *conducteur*.[3] And if he conducts and of course pushes those who are *in front of* him (the musicians), he also leads the auditors who are *behind*, like one pulls or tows a train. This is why his experience, in the visionary description Canetti gives, is so close to that of the child "followed on his own path" (about whom I dream, in the margins of Benjamin's fragment, that he, too, animates voices, silences others, gives them life or death, magically, *effictively*); this is why the action of the conductor also includes, as one of his essential components, a "making noise behind himself."

But the correspondence of these two experiences does not end there.

This is because the back of a modern orchestra conductor, this back he turns to the listeners, is the place of a functional transfer that disturbs the opposition between front and behind. Adorno said, "The conductor acts like the tamer of the orchestra, even though, through a mechanism of displacement, it is the audience he is aiming at."[4] And it's true, we could not understand the role of the conducting (or conductor's) body if we do not see within him a certain "indifference to the categories of front and behind." It is all in effect as if, on the other side of a symphonic décor that presents a sequence of *fronts* [*devantures*] (the audience looking at the conductor looking at the musicians) and acting *in the backs* of this ceremony that is as audible as it is visible, another operation were being inscribed, another traction or negotiation, the mirror of the one working its way through the obverse. And what is thus at stake on both sides of the conductor, what is at stake on the one side and the other, is nothing other than that fabrication of a collective body, the musical manufacture of a unified social organism, aggregating the disparateness of the members playing—or listening. Here too, Adorno stated this after several others: The conductor, orchestra, and audience form "something like a microcosm, in which the tensions of society are repeated and can be concretely studied."[5]

But that's not all: The conductor's back is also the result of an organic evolution made of turns and turnarounds whose abyss we could never finish measuring. There is, in fact, a whole whirling, an entire *tropology* of conducting postures and organologies to which I will return in much more detail. Here, I will simply note, as a provision, that one of the distant ancestors of contemporary conductors, the *chironomer*, was able to unfurl his manual gestures in an entirely different configuration of fronts and backings: chironomy—that art of directing music with hand signals seen in all the cultures of antiquity and all the way through Gregorian chant—survives and was still used recently within certain Jewish communities of Tunisia and Egypt, in a singular modality that consists in helping readers, in their melodic recitation of the Torah, by using the fingers to inscribe signs ("neumes") *onto their backs*.[6]

CHAPTER 19 Genesis (2): *Fantasia*, or "Plasmaticity"

An insert, once again, on childhood, and on the orchestra conductor. A few words, as an aside, on their bodies, both so plastic, before returning to the different forms of conduction or contagion that they call us to think.

In his surprising work on Walt Disney, Sergei Eisenstein associated the *animated* cartoon with the *animism* that "primitive man"—or the child—"confers upon inanimate nature."[1]

The childhood of art, then, or the art of childhood—and the birthing of the world.

Disney's *animations* are thus traced back to what Eisenstein calls the "phase of magical intercommunication with nature": the spectator, he says, is "restructured" in this, she is "brought back" to the "magical phase of the vision of the world."[2] A return [*remontée*] made possible by the great art of *editing* [*montage*].

Disney is said to thus take bodies away toward what remains inscribed in their "cell tissue," to what Eisenstein also calls their "plasmaticity," which does not have a "stable form" (15). Of course, he notes, one will have trouble acknowledging that the spectator has "recollection . . . of personally having existed" at the stage of "the beginning of its fetus-life" or "further down the evolutionary ladder." "But . . ." nothing is less certain, especially if one stops to think this in the terms of conscious memories: "Who," asks Eisenstein, "can take the measure of memory's 'base' this way, as it resides not only in the brain but also in each of the brain's predecessors, all the way back to the simple cell tissue?"

Eisenstein wasn't certain that he liked *Fantasia*. "*Fantasia*—is two-headed," he declared. "It's good when in the Disney realm there is the grotesque equivalent of music . . . bad when it is serious or dramatic" (79).

The bad *Fantasia* is the one of the first images. That of the demiurgic conductor: Leopold Stokowski, who, with all kinds of pathetic gestures, directs his orchestration of Bach's *Toccata and Fugue* in D minor, and who, against the backdrop of a solar circle, lights up the colors of the orchestra's instruments one by one. It is in effect serious and dramatic. The conductor is God; not without recalling Kircher's distant fable of Genesis, he is the one who seems to color the families of instruments according to correspondences between timbres and tints that are tainted, to say the least.

Once he disappears from the screen, however, once he and his kitschy sun disappear, the good *Fantasia* emerges. It's an abstract sequence that then goes by (it was, people say, largely responsible for the film's lack of success); it's an experiment that certainly conserves some trace of the brief and stormy collaboration with Oskar Fischinger, whom Disney had originally recruited for the project. It is here that Disney's declaration—"You will be able to *see* the music and *hear* the picture"[3]—it is here that this slogan that again bears such resemblance to Kircher is the least out of place. From a kind of primordial chaos, we watch the birth of lines, moving forms that sketch out the rhythms and motifs of Bach's fugue, forms that soon evoke organ pipes from which fireworks burst. A story—but without narration—of the simple musical genesis of forms in movement, which must indeed carry the memory of some archaic plasticity of bodies.

Eisenstein had also been interested in the unprecedented technical apparatus that accompanied the first projections of *Fantasia.*

It is in effect also through the technical invention of a new system of diffusion (later baptized *Fantasound*) that Disney was able to work toward a certain plasticity or plasmaticity of sound, as he himself explained with pride in a note he had sent around to his collaborators during a production meeting in 1938:

> All about the theaters will be concealed loudspeakers. Thus, for example, we can get the effect of the music marching about the theater, coming from the ceiling, one theme moving in one direction, a second theme circling the theater in the opposite direction, all meeting at the back of the theater.[4]

This properly *plastic* conformation or deformation of music *in the space of the theater* is something that Eisenstein also wanted to realize, in his staging of the *Valkyrie* for the Bolshoi in 1940. Nothing of this remains but his a posteriori description:

> I wanted to realize a variation on the "fusion" of the actor and the spectator. I imagined the "sonorous embrace" of the audience and wanted for the Wagnerian music to be able to enclose the spectator at the most pathetic height of the action. In order to do so, all down the hallways surrounding the theater, I wanted to place a system of speakers that would allow the music from the *Ride of the Valkyries*

literally to "melt" from one place to another and to be diffused at different moments from different corners of the theater before rumbling and resounding from everywhere all at once as an apotheosis, entirely abandoning the spectator to the power of the sound of the Wagnerian orchestra. I never had the chance to realize this project and continue to regret it today. In collaboration with Stokowski Disney later performed an experiment like this: in a theater, he demonstrated the effect of "stereophony" by presenting *Fantasia.* In a way absolutely analogous to what I had imagined, the spectator was placed at the intersection of several loudspeakers.[5]

Magical, plasmatic manipulation, where music is thrown and projected [*jetée, projetée*] into the "indifference to the categories of front and behind."

CHAPTER 20 Touching from Afar

As is the case for the gambler taken up in circles of suggestion, the radiance of the orchestra conductor in front and behind, the *conductive* capacities of his or her body must be deduced from the singular organology of the hand and its extensions.

Orchestra conducting has a long, complex history. It, too, is punctuated by the manufacture of unprecedented instruments, particularly keyboards, around which new, mobile innervations are woven. But this weave no longer only brings together feet, hands, and fingers: It also carries away the construction of the being-together of bodies into the melee of their *collective*. These are the *effictions* of the social body and its ties.

Must we recall it once again? Between *fiction* and *fabricating* [*faire*], there is more than an etymological kinship. *Factum-fictum*: Facts are fabricated.[1]

A certain fiction, thus a certain fabrication of the collective, may have begun—if it did begin one day—on the ancient *orchestra*, in that space that was the first theater of ritual trance or mania for the Greeks and which, much later on, gave its name to an ensemble of musicians who are united as one body.

The word *orchestra* is found in the writing of Plato and Aristotle where it designates the space that hosts the dances of the chorus; and the theater was probably born there from the fixation and codification of a ritual trance.[2] But it is difficult, if not impossible, to draw a thread from this that would lead to the modern Western orchestra. The use of the word *orchestra* presents in effect more discontinuities than coherences.[3] At the beginning of the seventh century, Isidore of Seville uses it for the stage itself (*Etymologiae*, 18:44). Then, with a few exceptions, the word seems to disappear from the medieval lexicon before reemerging around 1700 to name the space where musicians play. Thus, Johannes Mattheson wrote, "People wanted to honor the place where these gentlemen the symphonists have their place with the name of orchestra [*mit dem Namen Orchestre beehren*]." This phrase is found in his work published in Hamburg in 1713 and whose title—*Das neu-eröffnete Orchestre*—indicates in addition a more general meaning for this "still not very common expression [*noch nicht sehr gemeine*]," including "music both religious and theatrical, both vocal and instrumental [*beides Kirchen- und Theatral- so wol Vocal- als Instrumental-Musik*]." If this extension of the word's meaning seems to have remained a kind of hapax, on the contrary, its modern use to designate the place occupied by the "symphonists" settles in little by little: The eleventh volume of Diderot's *Encyclopedia* does not mention it in 1765, but Rousseau's *Dictionary of Music*, which appeared several years later, affirms in the article "Orchestre" that "at present, this word is more particularly applied to music, and means sometimes . . . the collection of all the symphonists."[4] The name is thus transferred from the space occupied by the musicians to their very collective.

We see that historical or etymological research does not allow us to draw a conclusion about any continuity between the ancient *orchestra* welcoming the evolutions of the chorus and the modern symphonic orchestra. But beyond this discontinuity in the use of the word, one question remains: From the Middle Ages to the eighteenth century, does the absence of a term to characterize the *totality* of the collective body of musicians not indicate an entirely different form of listening for which the sum of sound singularities is not yet a globalizing *fusion*? Or else, and correlatively: Does the late resurgence of the word to name the whole formed by a philharmonic symphony not bring about and accompany a certain return to what, on reflection, strongly resembles a relation of ritualized possession between the orchestra conductor and his or her musicians?

For there to be possession from afar between them, and without any intervention from a spirit exterior to the ceremony, there must be a spacing of bodies.

Little by little, the orchestra conductor will have had to detach himself from the collective organism, will have had to stand up and face it. He alone, standing up.

Bach still directed his musicians from the very heart of the orchestra, playing with and among them, at times the part of the keyboard, at others the first violin. This is how his son Carl Philipp Emanuel describes him in a letter to Forkel, Bach senior's biographer, in 1774: "In his youth, and until the approach of old age, he played the violin with a pure, piercing tone, and thus kept the orchestra under better control than he could have done with the harpsichord."[5] In other accounts, one nonetheless gets the sense that, despite his situation *in media res*, taken up in the melee of bodies, the conducting body has acquired a stature and centrality that only better redistributes the forces and signals he picks up. Here, for example, is what a certain Gesner, former rector of Saint Thomas, said of Bach at the keyboard in his accolade published in 1738:

> If you could see him, I say, . . . watching over everything and bringing back to the rhythm and the beat, out of thirty or even forty musicians [*symphoniaci*], the one with a nod, another by tapping with his foot, the third with a warning finger . . .—all alone, in the midst of the greatest din made by all the participants, and, although he is executing the most difficult parts himself, noticing at once whenever and wherever a mistake occurs, . . . full of rhythm in every part of his body—this one man taking in all these harmonies with his keen ear and emitting with his voice alone the tone of all the voices.[6]

It is at roughly the same time that, in France, the strange figure of the time beater [*batteur de mesure*] appears. In his pamphlet called "The Little Prophet of Boehmischbroda," telling of an evening spent at the Paris Opéra in 1753, F. W. von Grimm describes him in ironic terms as a kind of "woodcutter" (as the title of the pamphlet's fourth chapter has it):

> And I saw a man who was holding a stick, and I believed that he was going to castigate the bad violins. . . . . And he made a noise as if he were splitting wood, and I was astonished that he did not dislocate his shoulder, and the vigor of his arm terrified me. . . . And I beheld that they called that "beating the time," and although it was beaten most forcibly, the musicians were never together.[7]

André Ernest Modeste Grétry also mentions this noisy beater in his *Mémoires, ou Essais sur la musique* (1789) by acknowledging his necessity in conducting the many members and complex scenic changes that characterize the genre of French opera created by Lully (who in fact died, it is said, of complications from the hit of a stick dealt by himself on his own foot while conducting his *Te Deum* on January 8, 1687). All while criticizing its institution, Grétry paints the portrait of the conductor in a lexicon that is already that of a certain *fluid*, promised, as we will see, to a prosperous future:

> The slightest gesture, the smallest hit with his stick or his foot, is sensed by everyone; it's a fluid that is communicated to all the corners of an orchestra, whatever its size. . . . Except in the big choruses, where I think it is necessary for the theater, he is detrimental for proper execution. . . . It is . . . clear that symphonists become cold and indifferent when they do not directly follow the actor; the stick directing them humiliates them, takes away the emulation natural to every man who, able to obey his principal guide, sees himself constrained to follow the law of a third. The *bâton de mesure* is, however, necessary for opera theater where often, backstage, great choruses are performed when the dramatic situation demands it. One must not believe that a group of singers at this kind of remove can hear the orchestra, however numerous its members: Each singer sings in his neighbor's ear. . . . The chorus master can step forward and cast a glance on the baton, you will say; that's what he does: But if it is a dancing and singing chorus; if a crowd of dancers occupies downstage, the stick cannot be seen. The *batteur de mesure* then strikes against his stand, which is very unpleasant to hear; for he immediately reminds you that you are at the theater.[8]

Faced with the increase in members, the *batteur de mesure*, who proceeds from them, will soon himself become insufficient for ensuring cohesion. If it is the proliferation of sound-producing bodies and their dispersion in space that necessitate what Balzac, in *Le Cousin Pons*, will in 1847 call "the tyranny of the baton," it is this same proliferation that overflows it and leads it into competition with other apparatuses of command. Grétry already imagines a technical solution, an unprecedented piece of equipment to ensure the complicity better than the mere conducting baton can do:

> I have often thought about the ways to rectify this inconvenience; I think that it could be done, by placing a few fat organ pipes backstage or under the theater itself, by opening the floor through holes where the pipes are placed; the keyboard would be in the orchestra, an organist would touch it to accompany and guide the choruses and to keep them from leaving the tone.[9]

In these lines, Grétry literally echoes the incredible machinery (that he may not have known) unleashed during a "festival" in Handel's memory, organized at Westminster Abbey in 1784 and bringing together 525 singers and instrumentalists, all directed from the harpsichord. According to the testimony of the organizer of this monster-festival,[10] the harpsichord, in order to be heard by all, had been linked to the keyboard of an organ situated almost 600 meters away—and therefore activated from a distance.

The romantic orchestra conductor, with his miniature baton that seems to be an atrophied survival of the woodcutter's tool,[11] imposes himself little by little in the majority of European orchestras over the course of the first decades of the nineteenth century. And he, too, with his gesturing that conserves something of an old-new telesthesia, will sometimes see himself linked to apparatuses entirely like the one at the Handel "festival."

Thus, during the 1855 Universal Exhibition, Berlioz uses an "electric metronome" to "conduct" the 1,200 instrumentalists and choristers he had brought together; he describes its mechanism in minute detail:

> It consists of a set of copper wires connecting a battery underneath the stage to the conductor's stand and then on to a moving baton pivoted at one end on a board *at any distance* from the conductor. On the conductor's stand is fixed a copper key rather like a piano key. . . . As the conductor presses the copper key with his left index finger (his right hand is holding the baton), the key goes down, a weak electric spark is given off, and the baton at the other end of the copper wire oscillates on its board. Communication through the fluid to the moving baton is completely instantaneous, however far it has to travel. Performers in a group backstage with their eyes on the electric metronome's baton are thus directly in touch with the conductor's indications; if he needed to, he could conduct a piece played at Versailles from the middle of the orchestra of the Paris Opera.[12]

Here, we can see the idea take shape [*prendre corps*] that the one who conducts or directs the musical vehicle gets his powers from a physiochemical capacity of *electric conduction*. Even though it has rarely been remarked, this idea is omnipresent in the nineteenth century; it haunts this piece of writing as it does many other contemporary or later ones. Berlioz says nothing different when he states, on the basis of experience, the singular qualities necessary to the *conductor* that he, too, was:

> The conductor must be able both to see and to hear; he must be agile and energetic; he must know the construction,

> principles, and range of the instruments; he must be able to read a score and must have, besides the special talent whose ingredients we shall attempt to describe, other almost indefinable gifts without which an invisible bond cannot be struck between him and those whom he directs; without them the ability to convey his feelings to them is missing, and consequently the power, control, and direction will slip from him completely. . . . The musicians must feel that he feels, understands, and is moved. His feelings and emotions will then pass to them, his inner flame will warm them, his electricity will charge them, his drive will propel them. He will radiate the vital spark of music.[13]

The conductor is a fascinating telepathic machine. A machine to fascinate, quite precisely. And with galvanism.

One could certainly think that electricity here is only one metaphor among others, as in this obscure article by the correspondent from the *Allgemeine musikalische Zeitung*, giving an account of a concert that Louis Spohr had performed in London in 1820. The author explains that the English "call the accompanist on the pianoforte a 'conductor,' like a 'lightning conductor.'"[14] Is this lightning conductor leading the lightning onto the musicians just a joke? Is it simply, for lack of a better solution, a colorful possible lexicon to speak of "almost undefinable gifts," of the "invisible tie," of the "irradiations" that the conductor throws and projects around him?

Quite the contrary, I believe that electric conduction *literally* states what happens. It is while being veritably electrified or galvanized that orchestras—even and above all the most hypertrophied ones—constitute the organic body described by the organizer of the 1784 Handel "festival": "The pulsations in every limb, and ramifications of veins and arteries in an animal, could not be more reciprocal, isochronous, and under the regulation of the heart, than the members of this body of Musicians under that of the *Conductor*."[15]

It is the completion of this magnetic animal and the organic ties of the collective that can be read, in anticipation, in the utopic short story Berlioz publishes in 1852, "Euphonia, or the Musical City":

> An ingenious mechanism, which could have been invented five or six centuries earlier if someone had taken the trouble to design it, and which is actuated by the conductor without being visible to the public, indicates to the eye of each performer, and quite close to him, the beats of each measure. It also denotes precisely the several degrees of *piano* or *forte*. In this way the performers are immediately and instantaneously in touch with the conductor's intention, and can respond to it as promptly as do the hammers of a piano under the hand pressing the keys. The master can then say with perfect truth that he is *playing the orchestra*.[16]

What takes, precipitates, or materializes here is indeed that "fluid" Grétry was talking about and which, he said, "is communicated to all the corners of an orchestra, whatever its size." The conductor has become a kind of tele-keyboardist, transmitting from afar a flow about which we do not know—about which nothing allows us to say—if it metaphorically designates the glaring energy received, or, literally, the current that prolongs it toward the musicians. And, from the back, toward the audience. Instant radiation of the *actio in distans*. Or better yet: touching, commotion at a distance.

It is an unprecedented *collective body* [*faire-corps*] that is thus constructed in the symphonic music of the nineteenth century, parallel to the orchestra musicians' plunge into anonymity. (Earlier they were generally mentioned individually on concert programs.)[17]

Now, this new era of the collective body [*faire-corps*]—whose coming is tightly connected to the emergence of the "transcendent" orchestra conductor who plays the instrumentalists from a distance, as if through telepathy or magnetism—this era is also that of early statistics, which will overturn the image of the collective. Thus, in works of sociology, one sees figures borrowed from musical conduction flourish, as in this passage from the sociologist Gabriel Tarde, who evokes statistics as a kind of organ for the perception and control of "collections of similar units" that individuals have become:

> Consequently, granted that statistics be extended and completed to this extent, if the information it gives us continues to be perfected, accelerated, regularized, and increased, there may come a moment when . . . a statistical bureau might be compared to an eye and ear. Like the eye or ear, it would save us trouble by synthesizing collections of scattered homogenous units for us, and it would give us the clear, precise, and smooth result of this elaboration. . . . Let us hope that the day will come when the representative or legislator who is called upon to reform the judiciary or the penal code and yet who is, hypothetically, ignorant of juridical statistics, will be as rare and inconceivable a being as . . . a deaf orchestral leader would be to-day.[18]

Statistics are thus, as Tarde also says, "social physiology"; its offices have "ears." And here, too, this is not at all by chance; there is nothing that can be reduced to a mere language game, to a fortuitous and quickly dismissed coincidence among the words. As proof of this I offer a portrait of the orchestra conductor that appeared in an illustrated encyclopedia published starting in 1840 and titled *Les Français peints par eux-mêmes*

(The French depicted by themselves) (on which Balzac also collaborated); its author, a certain Alfred Legoyt, who played an important role in the development of the aforementioned "social statistics," also speaks of the conductor as a body "submitted to a kind of galvanism of singular power":

> To him in effect does this very complicated system of diverse modulations that make up harmony come to be connected; to him, like the foyer of an immense ellipse, does the noise of these formidable voices come to be reflected, which, multiplied by the echoes of the hall, play the great drama of the symphony from one end of the orchestra to the other. . . . Watch: Everything in him is animated and takes on a double life; he straightens up, sits back down, and gets back up; his foot, hand, and head are as many electric currents for which his magic wand seems to serve as conductor.[19]

If one sees him with the weave of the conductive ties that prolong his hand, the orchestra conductor gives figure to the collective as a unity of anonymous units forming a body. And if, as Adorno wrote in a somewhat hastily condescending way, the orchestra conductor is saddled with "magical qualities," if he is endowed with the "healer's power of fascination,"[20] there is something entirely different from a mere belief here, from which one might quickly believe oneself sobered or delivered. The *ties*, the *threads* that are woven through and through among the conducting and conducted bodies are lastingly active; they do not wait to be invested with meaning or soul or spirits; they *are* the reality of bodies that music ties together, assembles, shapes, composes, and deposes. In other words, fictions [*fictionne*].

CHAPTER 21 **Organologics (3): Areality**

Areality, writes Jean-Luc Nancy, "is an antique word, signifying the nature or specificity of an *aire* [area]." And, he adds, "By chance, this word also serves to suggest a lack of reality, or rather a slight . . . reality."[1]

Shaping, fictioning, or assembling bodies that, distributed in space, hold together and even to themselves merely through threads—threads of ligatures [*liaisons*], threads of innervations and fibers, threads of fictions, threads of conduction—this is what music *does* and proposes. Gathering these areal but in no way unreal bodies into a discourse that disposes of them (and that redisposes them), this is what a general organology should keep in sight.

Such was the project of André Schaeffner; such were the ambitions to which his *Origine des instruments de musique* attempted to hold. One could never celebrate his project too much.[2]

The organologist and anthropologist chooses to recount the opening of a spatiality and a technicity in music—in the art of time and the art of the body that it is—as a genealogical narrative. Reading Schaeffner, one thus gets the impression that, since the dawn of time, there has been a kind of continual *exudation* from the human body. ("*Exsudation*," the French Littré dictionary tells us, is a term in physiology: "seepage of a humor through the walls of its natural reservoir.") So it seeps sound prostheses: On the one hand, limbs at their ends give birth to musical instruments, and, on the other, cavities of organic resonance are externalized in resonators and other objectively constituted spaces (in "theaters," for example).

In effect, for Schaeffner "instrumental music, in its most primitive forms, always presupposes dance": "Man hits the ground with his feet or his hands, beats his body in rhythm, or else shakes a part or all of it in order to move the sound objects and ornaments it carries" (13–14). According to an essentially continual genealogy, it is then "a cluster or strings of objects tied around the body that dance" (39), giving birth to "a dance of objects that rustle . . . all along a handle" shaken by a hand (53). Exteriorization or exudation. Instrumentality literally *expresses itself*; it *pushes* and *presses* to erupt, protuberant and prosthetic, through the walls of the body-reservoir. It is still according to this same physiological genealogy that theater, for Schaeffner, is a matter of organology. In the Homeric era, he writes, the *orchestra* "first designated the places that resonated under our steps." And this *organology of the theater*, as he calls it, is not an exclusively Western prerogative, far from it. It is even not far from being a universal aspect of the evolution of musical technologies:

> Like Greek drama, Japanese *nô* has its origin in dance; it inaugurates the theater by covering the primitive place for dance with a wooden platform . . . ; the hardwood floor vibrates and its sound is reinforced thanks to earthenware jars that are placed beneath it. . . . If the stage floor can be a sound board, how could we not admit that the whole theater forms a vast resonator and that its structure is like that of the instruments? (88–90)

This filiation that, through exudation and exteriorization, leads continuously from the "proper" (or human) body to the acoustic spaces with complex dispositions that theaters are has something fascinating about it. Its beauty and force is no doubt in its organicist and anthropocentric presupposition: We, we humans, are thought to have given birth to instrument spaces that are the prolongations of our body and its organs, with ramifications that are certainly complex but with no solution of continuity.

Yet we should also reserve rights to another perspective, according to which the instrument and its spatiality would structurally move beyond, so to speak, the span of "man." (The "span" [in French *empan*] is, according to Littré, a sewing term that designates the distance between the two arms.) Perhaps "man" becomes sonorous only by becoming instrumental himself, in other words by becoming a spatial distribution of himself to himself. There would, therefore, be no need to suppose a "proper" sonorous body becoming increasingly instrumental and exteriorized, right up to the fatal moment of the loss of contact and dispossession that, in this perspective, does not delay in irrupting like a *technical* misfortune or accident that affects the anthropocentric chain of evolution.[3] We should rather turn our thoughts to modes of coupling excitation with resonance thanks to which, each time in a singular, more or less inaugural way, bodies (the "proper" one and the prosthetic one) are articulated for a *conjoint* sonorous becoming—in their very disjunction and distribution in space.

We would, therefore, need to say that it is a general and original instrumentality that disposes the human to the sonorous. That puts him outside himself in order to *make sound*. For no doubt "my" body does not become sonorous, properly sonorous (in other words resonant) until it goes through the experience of a kind of disarticulation of self through which a member or an area "detaches" itself to become the space of resonance of others. When I produce "corporeal music" by beating my chest, my body is already not entirely *my* body. It is already at a distance from itself. It has *arealized* itself. In other words, it has distributed itself into *areas* and disjointed surfaces. It has already split into clappers and resonating cavities. Even the voice finds its origin in the echo of all the different kinds of tubes and hollows where my body subtracts in part from itself to come and resonate there as a "sonorous body." From this point of view, there is no essential difference between the voice projected for itself and a horn. Not to mention the "crystal voice" (the Mongol *höömii*), in which the tongue selects the overtones produced by the buccal cavity as a finger would on a violin's fingerboard, or of the Inuit *katajjaq*, in which the resonating body is nothing other than the other's mouth.

To state that there is no *essential* difference between a voice and a horn, or between a beaten chest and a skin drum, does not mean mixing all producers of sound together under the general sign of instrumentality. On the contrary, recognizing that any sonorous body (whether "proper" or "artificial") is a matter of an articulation among arealities that is both conjunctive and disjunctive means opening a space of thought and experience that welcomes the sometimes epochal differences among these couplings. It means in any case breaking both with any simple opposition between nature and technique and with all continuist perspectives that seem to make an appeal to body-prosthesis continuity only the better to postpone the breaking point (which in general emerges only with much more violence or insistence).[4] To say that any sonorous body is originally arealized means giving up on any privilege of figures of proximity or contact; it means being able to think through the most disjunctive and distant articulations or couplings, not as accidents or misfortunes (according to I don't know what kind of technophobic fatalism that is as common as its technophilic twin), but as differences in their own right, without a nostalgic gaze turned toward a lost *original and corporeal essence.*

Thinking the original areality of musical bodies also opens, according to the chance inscribed in this fine word, onto new organological perspectives for what is often called, in a confused and incantatory way, *virtual reality.*

CHAPTER 22 **Bodies Electric**

The era of this specific unlinking of sonorous bodies through which we are currently living, *this* singular era, was no doubt inaugurated by electricity.

The figures, postures, and dispositions of the orchestra conductor, with his galvanism and *tactus in distans*, are marked by it.

But what electricity also little by little allows to emerge in its nudity is the original spacing that disposes bodies to *making sound* by exposing them to one another as resonators.

Around 1730, Prokop Diviš, a priest from Bohemia, begins to construct the first musical instrument involving electricity, of which we know very little. In his *Biographie universelle des musiciens* published in 1874, François-Joseph Fétis simply relates that, around 1730, "Diwisch [*sic*] imagined the lightning rod, whose invention was later found by Franklin, and a kind of *Orchestrion*, a big musical instrument, to which he gave the name *Denis d'or*, by analogy with his own, which signifies *Dennis*, in Bohemian." And Fétis adds: "This instrument was played, like the organ, with the hands and the feet; it imitated, they say, all the string and wind instruments, and we can be assured that it could produce one hundred thirty varieties of qualities of sound."[1]

With the *clavecin électrique* produced by the Jesuit Jean-Baptiste Delaborde in 1750, static electricity becomes an essential component of an instrument whose mechanism is described with precision by its inventor. In the first of his *Letters on the Electric Harpsichord*, Delaborde describes his apparatus through an analogy with the organ:

> Electrical matter is its soul just as air is the Organ's. The globe [where static electricity has built up] takes the place of the bellows, & the conductor that of the wind chest. In the organ, *the keyboard is like a brake* with which one moderates the action of the air. I imposed the same brake onto electrical matter, in spite of its subtlety and agility. The air held in the Organ's wind chest moans there until the Organist, like Aeolus, opens the gates of his prison. If he were to get rid of all the barriers that stop him, this would create terrible confusion and disorder; but he knows how to give it *different ways out* with discernment. Electrical matter thus remains captive, as it were, and trembles uselessly around the bells of the new Harpsichord, until it is set free by lowering the keys. It then escapes at the highest speed; but it stops acting as soon as the keys are raised.[2]

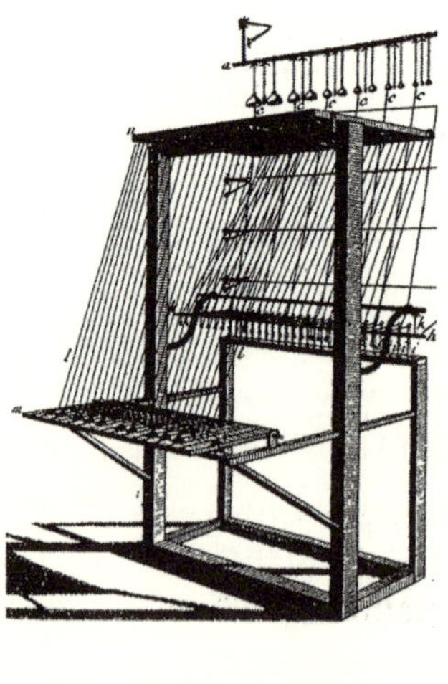

The organ—the ancient one, the very first of the "mechanical" instruments, whose invention is in fact contemporary with the keyboard—is conceived of here as a group of reservoirs of energy that it is a matter of stopping rather than starting, whose escape must be mastered. And it is according to this model that the instrument producing sound will become a machine harboring a *circulation* (of fluids and forces) rather than a mechanism that works according to excitation and resonance.

But unlike the organ's circuits (be they hydraulic or pneumatic), those of the "electric harpsichord" are no longer structurally limited in length.[3] This is why, with electricity, musical instruments inaugurate a new regime of the coupling of bodies where the distance between them is potentially infinite. In other words, it is on the basis of the electrification of sonorous bodies that the articulation of musical arealities is absolutely untied from any organic or geographical unity (local, punctual, compact). It is no longer a question of greater or lesser proximity or distance: The dislocation is radical. And at that point, as we will see, the organology of theater, as Schaeffner would say, also opens itself to a new spatiality. With electricity, the instrument and the theater of its amplification truly become *networks* whose limbs, if I may put it this way, hang by a thread.[4]

However, for these structural possibilities to be realized in effectively unprecedented arealities, one has to wait for electricity to be applied to telegraphy, and later to the telephone.

It is surprising to note that experiments with the transmission of music from a distance were undertaken before the telephone was developed.[5] Thus, already in the 1870s, the American inventor Elisha Gray developed systems of multiplex (or *harmonic*) telegraphy capable of transmitting several simultaneous messages coded for different frequencies along the same cable. The transmitters—oscillating steel reeds tuned differently, activated by electromagnets and interrupting the current at specific frequencies—looked like keyboards able to cover up to two octaves. Gray presented one of these apparatuses during a concert in Chicago in 1874.[6]

Alexander Graham Bell, the inventor of the telephone in 1876, was also experimenting with apparatuses of multifrequency telegraphy. And the very year he developed the telephone, he organized the first long-distance concert: The voices of three singers were transmitted over telegraphic cables between two cities in Ontario: Paris and Brandtford. A year later, on April 2, 1877, it was Gray's turn to present a concert at the Steinway Hall in New York. Frederick Boskowitz, a famous pianist, played on a telegraphic transmitter with twelve keys in the Western Union offices in Philadelphia, while the New York audience lent an ear to this music that came from nowhere.[7]

In these dislocations that inaugurate a new spatiality of music, it is the traditional notion of *instrument* that is smashed into pieces. Gray's experiments with diverse receptors testify to this. In effect, he tried to attach electromagnets to the sound box of a violin, to metal boxes, to little drums. For his April 1877 telegraphic concert, he used sixteen wooden tubes calibrated in length, hollow, and resonating. And this apparatus, to which an electromagnet communicated signals received at a distance, was mounted on a Steinway perhaps serving as a supplementary sound box within the vast space of Steinway Hall.

We see here that it is, *conjointly*, both the unity of space of the concert *and* the organological—or better organic—unity of the instrument that explodes. Or rather, the more arealizing technicity is implicated in music, the more the original structure that brings together excitation, resonance, and amplification, already secretly present in every primitive sonorous body, *is exposed as such*. Is arealized.

This type of long-distance concert soon spread to Europe.[8] Thus was Clément Ader able to organize stereophonic concerts by telephone in the Parisian context of the International Exposition of Electricity in 1881. Transmitters had been hung all along the projectors on either side of the whisperer on stage at the Paris Opera House. Telephone lines had been strung along two kilometers, linking the opera house to the Palais de l'Industrie, in the exposition. There, the auditors had pairs of receptors available that were connected to transmitters differently placed on the opera stage in order to ensure the spatial (i.e., stereophonic) replication of the concert and of the movements of the singers. The first work to be transmitted this way was Meyerbeer's *Robert le Diable*. Starting in 1882, Theodor Puskás organized similar events in Budapest.

In 1897 an inventor by the name of Thaddeus Cahill filed the patent for an apparatus exclusively and specifically destined *to distribute music from a distance*. In this patent, the telharmonium (or dynamophone) is described as a machine "to generate music electrically with tones of good quality and great power and with perfect musical expression, and to distribute [this] music . . . from a central station to translating instruments located at different points and all receiving their music from the same central point."[9]

The telharmonium was a giant instrument, a veritable "electric power plant of sounds."[10] Installed in New York in 1906 in order to be used commercially, the instrument gave daily concerts that subscribers could hear transmitted across a distance through cables. People dined to the sound of the telharmonium. And some newspapers from the time testified in their own ways to the upheaval of the soundscape spatiality that confuses the usual borders that had, up until then, contained music within specific contexts. Since the cables installed for the telharmonium passed through the same conduits as those of the telephone, there was interference, with the consequences described by an article in the *New York Globe and Commercial Advertiser* in which the journalist speaks of "domestic incidents" caused by the telharmonium:

> It has even threatened to break up families. There is the case of a man who had to work late in his office one night, and called up his wife to tell her that instead of going home he would stay at a hotel. Just at that moment the merry strains of the "William Tell" overture came floating over the wires. "Where are you now?" his wife asked suspiciously. "In the office, of course," he made answer. "Indeed?" she replied. "Since when have you had an orchestra in your office? You're deceiving me. You're in some theatre. Don't try to deny it. I can hear the music."[11]

One can imagine the husband's confusion—a confusion that is anything but an isolated case. For the developments of musical teletechnology go hand in hand with an upheaval in the limits between *private* and *public*. One could find a thousand proofs of this. I offer only one, one that was related by a lawyer from the time who worked on the legal problems linked to the mechanization of music.[12] One night in 1890, while Johann Strauss was giving a concert at Madison Square Garden in New York, "a master of the house who was hosting an evening in Morristown was using as a ballroom music the orchestra playing twenty or thirty miles from there." And it's true, different judicial decisions will not delay in recording the new areality of this off-site music by clearly establishing that a long-distance transmission was a performance of the work.[13]

Touching on the areality of sonorous bodies means touching not only on the organology of theaters but also on all kinds of other spaces and borders: judicial, social, symbolic, and so on.

The continuation of this organological adventure that puts *both* theaters *and* instruments at stake (the instrument *as* a theater and the theater *as* an instrument) is the era of radio(tele)phony: in other words, the era (we are still in it) of the wireless or of the mobile.

The American engineer Lee de Forest was very early in proposing to place his system of "radiotelephony" at the service of the telharmonium. On February 28, 1907, in his diary, he made the following note:

> Radio Telephony and Teleharmony—new, epoch marking. . . . [I] seek to transmit these glorious vibrations of sound made by the new electricity, without a medium save that intangible, viewless, *bodiless* mystery of mysteries, the ether.[14]

It is according to the same radiophonic principle that, in 1919, Lev Theremin, a Russian physician, realized the "etherphone" that bears his name: One plays it by moving one's hands in front of an antenna. Theremin went on many tours in Europe. In an article published in German in 1927, he writes: "Thus, in the space surrounding the antenna is born *a kind of invisible fingerboard*; and in the same way that, on the cello, the finger that *presses down on* the string provokes a higher pitch as one nears the bridge, here, the sound rises as *one draws nearer to* the antenna."[15] Touch (pressure) becomes distant: It's an *approach*.

Theremin, sent on tour in Europe, presents a concert-lecture in Paris, first on December 6, 1927, at the Salle Gaveau, then two days later at the Paris Opera House. Commentary from a journalist at *Le Monde musical*: "The radioelectrical apparatuses constructed by M. Theremin truly touch on the limits of the marvellous. Not only do they give the possibility of making music with *a mere movement of the hands in space*, but they also allow the executant to give to the sound produced the timbre of very different wind and string instruments, and even of the human voice, in whatever quantities, and to perfection."[16]

The German press also broadly comments on the instrument. In 1927, in the journal *Funk*, Hans Böhm writes that it is easy to "turn the ether keyboard [*Ätherklavier*] into a normal radio";[17] one can even "receive and play [*konzertieren*] at the same time, that is, use the radio orchestra, for example, as an accompaniment for one's own musical solo practice." Theremin's etherphone thus promises a domestic musical practice of an entirely new kind, a *Hausmusik* that is not without announcing that "invention" that is dated to the beginning of the 1970s: karaoke, the Japanese term for *absent orchestra*. To unite an orchestra of etherphones, Böhm adds, it is not necessary to have "as many apparatuses, speakers, and batteries as of parts." Except for the antennae, everything else "can be shared," like today's electronic instruments connected in *networks*.

Theremin emphasizes that "the change in pitch and dynamic can be produced not only through the movement of the hands, but also by that of the whole body, *even at a certain distance from the apparatus*." And he adds that "this possibility opens a vast perspective for the problem of the relations between music and dance."[18] With its invisible key, with its sensitivity to the entire body, the etherphone is a kind of virtual musical space *avant la lettre*. This is the ultimate phase in the arealization of sonorous bodies (ultimate because I think that, despite all the later improvements and inventions, we are still *structurally* in Teremin's era). But, paradoxically, in the chain of organological mutations and disjunctions, this last link seems to have restored something along the lines of a fantasy of vocal or corporeal immediacy: At the very moment when cables, those last fragile threads materializing the articulation of exciters and resonators, are disappearing, it is also distance itself, and disjunction, that become *ungraspable*. By playing a Theremin, one not only plays in a space: According to a fiction of immediacy that is inherent in this "etherphone," one plays space. Without intermediary, without mechanism or key.

The areality of bodies, in its phase of extreme dislocation, inaugurates a new era—ours, already but not yet—of this *touching at a distance* that music is. Where we see the opening of the—fictive? effictive?—perspective of touching on everything without touching anything at all.

CHAPTER 23 Mass Formations

What could the future of these intangible bodies be? These telesthesias that are sketched out and resonate in a space without keys [*touches*]?

What old-new organologic is at work here, at this provisional end of a vast process of *unlinking* [*déliaison*]?

What is music still leaving, *right there*, as the suspended persistence of bodies that, one day perhaps, will effictively be ours?

We have come a long way.

When the medieval musical theory inherited from Boethius sees its corpus come apart (it was a corpus in which bodies held together, thanks to the world's *contextio*),[1] when instrumental music (in the specifically Western sense of the word) starts to make bodies that are closed and detached entities proliferate, bodies whose unity is in itself problematic, then "the body," that modern effiction, becomes the theater where we must reweave a lost contexture anew. Because given that the link between the macrocosm and the microcosm is irremediably undone, the Boethian categories of *musica mundana* and *musica humana* no longer sustain one another: There remains only a *musica instrumentalis* whose principle of ligature [*liaison*] is always missing (in Boethius it was already a more or less empty category).

Let's remember: Starting with the era of Virdung and then of Couperin, what was opening against a backdrop of the unlinking [*déliaison*] of sonorous bodies was precisely the injunction to link. To link, yes, what was one day unlinked, when the musicus began to cede his place to the idiot. And thus to compensate for this unlinking that emerged from the irruption of a discrete instrumental idiotism. In other words to phrase, as a way of spanning with the arc of a legato the defects, holes, and gaps that arealizing instrumental technicity—of which keyboards will have here been the emblem or the exemplary figure—digs out within the musical.

Yet as we have seen, phrasing means multiplying these similar and increasingly substitutable (and even infinitely tropical) unities of fingers, feet, organs, in short, the *members* of this "society" named body. Or "self."[2]

With the help of the development of an instrumental music long kept to one side and diabolized (it incarnated in effect division itself, the *dia-bolic*, literally), the musical body became a kind of black hole in which the unity of a cosmic, social, and organic order is continually imploding. In this black hole are found, *abîmés* (that is, both *mise en abyme* and deconstructed), the vestiges of a communitarian or societal contexture that some would like to see restored, anchored anew in an old-new *musica mundana*, in a "music of the spheres" for today.

In effect, the telharmony that has perhaps always haunted bodies is now exposed as such. And there is no lack of attempts that seek to draw a happy utopia from this late ramification of musical organology. This is the case—to take one example among others—of certain symphonic projects by the video artist Nam June Paik: for example, his *Symphony no.* 5, conceptualized at a time (1965) when he claimed to be close to both Stockhausen and Fluxus, and in which a certain harmony of the spheres seems to be seeking to take shape once again:

> Play the Grosse Fugue (op. 133) of L. V. Beethoven / first violin part on earth / second violin part on the moon / viola on Venus . . . / cello on Mars . . . starting exactly the first of July at 12:10 at noon . . . / (Greenwich mean time on earth)[3]

Paik's reference to Stockhausen, recurrent at the time of this "fifth symphony," is not by chance: After having multiplied the experiments in the delocalization of sound sources, Stockhausen, who is happy to describe sounds "as flying objects," went so far in his *Helikopter-Streichquartett* as to have the four members of a string quartet play in a cockpit transporting each one separately through the air; on earth, and at his console, the demiurgic composer mixed their four voices.[4]

These "scores" are utopic in the sense that they are never far from interpreting musical areality as lack of reality, as a non-place—in other words, as an area (for play) whose dislocation and unbinding would leave a space for a beyond. By projecting their telharmony into a space that seeks, at the limit, to be "worldwide" (or "global" on the scale of the globe), they explicitly or implicitly aim *beyond the world.*

In Stockhausen's work, this aim is explicit at least since the beginning of the 1970s and therefore even before the formulation of his project of dramatic heptalogy (the seven days of the monumental opera *Licht*, begun in 1977); his works, Stockhausen regularly declares, seek out "the immersion of the individual in the All of the cosmos."[5]

The resurgence of a totalizing *musica mundana* is of course less patent in the manifestos that accompany the happenings of the Fluxus movement, of which Paik was one of the major representatives. At first sight, the accent seems in effect to be placed on the *materiality* of the sonorous bodies, on their being-there rather than their being-over-there. George Maciunas, in one of the manifestos he wrote for Fluxus, could thus write:

> A note sounded on a piano keyboard or a belcanto voice is largely immaterial, abstract and artificial since the sound does not clearly indicate its true source or material reality—common action of string, wood, metal, felt, voice, lips, tongue, mouth etc. A sound, for instance, produced by striking the same piano itself with a hammer or kicking its underside is more material and concrete since it indicates in a much clearer manner the hardness of hammer, hollowness of piano sound box and resonance of string.[6]

But to this was immediately added: "Anti-art is life, is nature, is true reality—it is *one and all*" (emphasis mine). The material bodies thus quickly become glorious, if not celestial, bodies that draw their glory from their participation in the celebration of a totality yet to come. And the ceremony of the happening, as we know, takes on an air of sacrifice:[7] In his *Carpenter's Piano Piece for Nam June Paik no. 13*, Maciunas prescribes nailing the keys of a piano down; in another project by Paik, the musicians "push grand pianos, overturn a piano, the piano falls from the stage onto the floor of the concert hall,"[8] and in 1962, *One for Violin* celebrates the immolation of a violin.

Never will we have pursued the materiality of sonorous bodies as much as during the era of their dislocation, even though this desperate quest often makes of it, and with even more certainty, an ungraspable ideality. It would seem that the more we look for it by hypostatizing it, the more "the body" goes missing.

This is why the formula for these utopias is perhaps older than we might think. More than three centuries ago, Marin Mersenne was already wondering: "How strong must the voice be in order to be carried and heard all the way on the Moon, on the Sun, and in the firmament, either naturally, or through some artifice?"[9]

In one of his virulent critiques of symphonic practice (published under the title "Of Time and Time Beaters" and signed by the pseudonym Herbert von Hochmeister), Glenn Gould took on a kind of dark side of the figure of dislocation. Tying together into a terrifying knot the conductor's magnetism, areal unbinding, and autophony, he made a "gamble" that looks like a bad utopia—a *dystopia*—out of science fiction:

> The conducting of the future will be accomplished by a closed-circuit hypnotic-eye inspiration synthesizer, a democratically programmed compote of the interpretative ideas and ideals of all sidemen, managers, and critics everywhere. Its persuasive conception of the literature will be whammied to the sidemen in their acoustic-tiled studios, in which all rehearsing and performing will, of course, be done—blend, as such, being achieved at the master control by programming another set of a priori specifications. Thus, the orchestral player will take several giant steps into the automated future. He can stay home to perform.[10]

Let's forget the science fiction: As we know, this is indeed how pop music singers can, already today, record in Paris all while being accompanied live by a rhythm section playing in Los Angeles or a string orchestra set up in Dublin via high-speed broadband connection.[11] Berlioz, more modestly but in a premonitory way, dreamed only of a telharmonic conduction between Paris and Versailles. And who knows what is reserved for us by the developments yet to come from a worldwide musical network dominated by the major record labels and the music industry?

Rather than science fiction in its usual sense, Gould's "gamble" participates in a long chain of organological effictions that I have tried to trace out, and almost all of whose threads, right down to the wireless, converge here. Statistics, in this dystopia, is realized as what Gabriel Tarde only barely dared dream, in the conditional tense, when he wrote, "A statistical bureau might be compared to an eye and ear. . . . It would save us trouble by *synthesizing* collections of scattered homogenous units for us." In actuality, the Gouldian dystopia would be a kind of apotropaic staging, a veritable foil when confronted with the embodiment of this fiction of "perfect and absolute" sociality according to Tarde, which "would consist of such an intense concentration of urban life that as soon as a good idea arose in one mind it would be instantaneously transmitted to all minds throughout the city."[12] If, still according to Tarde, "the social like the hypnotic state is only a form of dream, a dream of command and a dream in action,"[13] if "social life" consists in "terraces of consecutive and connected magnetizations,"[14] one could then say that Gould very exactly produces its troubling musical effiction.

In the aftermath of the mutations that have punctuated the vast process of unlinking and dislocation initiated at least since Virdung, the Stockhausenian utopia and Gouldian dystopia are effictive extremes among the many that weave through the bodies of "our time," as well as their being-body. They only enflame, by taking them to the point of incandescence, the latent motifs of long-distance conduction, telharmony, and telesthesia. (And they brush up against the fantasy of a kind of *panacoustics* in which the designers of "panoptical" prisons, in the nineteenth century, could have seen the most appropriate crowning of their efforts.)[15]

In his lecture on telepathy, Freud, as you'll remember, had also let himself be if not quite fascinated then at least intrigued by the possibility of mastery of telesthesia ("only think if one could get hold of this physical equivalent of the psychical act!" he wrote). Yet at the end of the same conference, he declared:

> If only one accustoms oneself to the idea of telepathy, one can accomplish a great deal with it—for the time being, it is true, only in imagination. It is a familiar fact that we do not know how the common purpose comes about in the great insect communities: possibly it is done by means of a direct psychical transference of this kind. One is led to the suspicion that this is the original, archaic method of communication between individuals and that in the course of phylogenetic evolution it has been replaced by the better method of giving information with the help of signals which are picked up by the sense organs. But the older method might have persisted in the background and still be able to put itself into effect under certain conditions—for instance in passionately excited mobs.[16]

Archaic, stemming from a kind of collective trance, this "original" communication repressed by evolution may well find new life particularly in musical *conduction*. Adorno understood this very well, he who, in the pages he devoted to the orchestra conductor, mentions Freud's *Massenpsychologie* and his recourse to the notion of collective hypnosis.[17]

In this essay on mass psychology, Freud nonetheless advances an objection to the traditional sociological explanations of the behavior of the crowd through the capacity for suggestion or imitation that would be proper to them: "It seems difficult," he writes, "to attribute to the factor of number a significance so great as to make it capable by itself of arousing . . . a new instinct that is otherwise not brought into play."[18] This is why Freud attempts to *reduce the number*, to drive the analysis of the crowd onto the terrain proper to psychoanalysis, and particularly to the *reduced model of identification* (conceived of as a "link" to one, and only one, other). At the end of this research, whose awkwardness reveals the problem's immense difficulty without ever camouflaging it (it is a matter, no more and no less, of making a relation to others erupt from only the individual psyche),[19] Freud advances a paradoxical formulation: "The hypnotic relation is (if this expression is permissible) a group formation with two members."

Perhaps it is not entirely unjustified to deduce here, for my purposes, two final hypotheses. One would be that the developments of group telesthesia and telharmony, conduction and its equipment, were already virtually contained and prefigured *in nucleo* in the conformation or fabrication of a simple singular body grappling with an instrument—in other words, even before any consideration of a given collective (which would be only the development or prolongation of individual body-to-body contact). Or perhaps—second hypothesis—one would have to say on the contrary, with or without Freud, that something of the contagion in a crowd and of the domino effect of magnetizations was *already* operating in the singular compositions and apprehensions of bodies that Diderot or Marie Jaëll described. Was it not a chain of suggestions that, from Diderot to d'Alembert and beyond, propagated the effiction of a keyboard-body? Was it not the magnetism of a *crowd of fingers* that the pianist described while watching Liszt's arborescent hand?

Let's go even further. Or closer up, closer to the limbs.

When listening to music, it is not only that we perceive sonorous bodies, sonorous gestures, as Roland Barthes said of Schumann's *Kreisleriana*, in which he heard the thousand movements of a "body that beats."[20] It is also because, for someone who lends an ear with the microphonic and almost muscular attention of Couperin, one hears the *fingerings*, in other words, without necessarily having a clear consciousness of it, the construction and organization *in act* of a chain of relays from limb to limb: There is here something like "tactile form, a succession of muscular tensions" (to quote Ligeti's words about Chopin and his own *Etudes*);[21] it's a sequence of *articulations of organs*, on the stage of an organic microsociety where the forces, hierarchies, norms, and exceptions are infinitely put back into play, started over, renegotiated.

The literature for the keyboard is teeming with patent examples where this finger or that organ suddenly sees itself given a power and a role that radically reconfigure what Glenn Gould called the "tactile image" projected by music.[22] Let us recall Carl Philipp Emanuel Bach's fine pages devoted to the central reign of the thumb. Let us also remember how Chopin demanded, for each finger, the respect for its singularity under attack from the enterprise of military enlistment led by the Romantic school on this little digital society that one hand is.[23]

The *engagement* (in its energetic or political sense, as you like) of sonorous bodies starts *here*, I am convinced of this: *here*, in other words in the formation of the tiniest deviations from organ to organ, in the capacity for invention that works in the midst of the tiniest body-to-body contacts. Here where effictive phantom limbs grow.

Since the time of Virdung or Couperin, and including our contemporary telesthesiac unlinking, the question of what it might mean to *have* a body, without returning to the Boethian order, is entirely open. *Possessing* that "immense gathering" Nietzsche spoke of, these innumerable phantom limbs and organs, so effictive whenever music interprets them through my body-to-body contact with the instrument—this is the *abyss* that "I" experience every day when I sit down at the keyboard.

When, at the keyboard, "I embody" (as Heidegger so clearly put it when speaking of Nietzsche), when the bodies espouse one another—the resonant and multiplying body of the instrument but also the bodies of all those who will have left their traces on the claviature—"I" would already be exposed to the crowd. "I" would already be, in the body-to-body contact, *a group formation of two members.*

And it would thus be starting with the most singular body-to-body contact that the stakes of musical playing would become: how *to hold oneself*, even though one must indeed phrase, within unlinking as such? In other words, there is here, still to come, the horizon of the idiotism of the musical body. It is the fragile possibility that its idiotism be written and inscribed, without reactive or totalizing nostalgia, within a musical space that is arealized worldwide.

This position, at once tenuous and strong, right in the middle of what is hanging by only one thread, is something Thelonious Monk incarnated in an overwhelming way. This is why his idiom, by continuing to resist its becoming-language and being fixed within a corpus, still speaks to us today. This is why, for the future, we hear resonating in it something like an injunction to reinvent bodies, and being-bodies.

But I wouldn't want to close my attempt at a genealogy of sonorous organs without also mentioning the one that, more than any other *today*, to my eyes brings these stakes to the height of a veritable *musical engagement.* At least since the 1970s, the German composer Helmut Lachenmann has undertaken a deconstruction of musical organizations that makes each one of his works the theater of a micropolitics of bodies. Lachenmann works on sound with a heightened awareness that every note and every gesture carries the sediments of a glory he names "philharmonic" (and that for my part I would prefer to describe as telharmonic). He works *against* this, and *right up against* it.

With works like *Pression* (1970, for solo cello) or *Guero* (1970, for a piano whose keys and tuning pegs are scraped and rubbed, reminiscent of Monk's fingernails), Lachenmann sought to grasp instrumental sound "as the sign of its production," of its "energetic aspect." In an interview he granted me in 1993, the composer specified:

> This energetic aspect is not new, but in classical music, it had a more or less articulating function (the harp in Mahler's work as a deformed kettledrum, the brass in Bruckner's work like a superhuman lung, the high pizzicato of violins in the opening of Berlioz's *King Lear*, that Richard Strauss compared to an artery that exploded in the head of the sovereign . . .). . . . I placed it at the center of my musical conception. . . . Sound was thus no longer understood as an element to be varied under the aspect of the interval, harmony, rhythm, timbre, and so on, but above all as the result of applying a mechanical force under physical conditions that are controllable and variable through composition: the sound of the violin understood and regulated as the result of a characteristic friction between two characteristic objects, like one particular version among other modes of friction and other objects that, until then, did not belong to philharmonic practice.[24]

With *Ein Kinderspiel* (A children's game, 1981), Lachenmann drew the radical consequences of this manner of proceeding to where they were least expected: in the "pedagogical" literature for the piano. Here too the energetic or corporeal "background" of the sound "moves to the foreground": "We don't hear song over a piano, but piano over a song [*wir hören nicht ein Lied auf dem Klavier, sondern wir hören Klavier auf einem Lied*]," he declares.[25] And, in fact, the simple melodic or rhythmic structures, like a nursery rhyme or a jig, become the bases or the skeletons over which unfurl all the variants of resonance of that great body the piano is. Generalizing Schumann's intuitions,[26] Lachenmann, in some of his little études, makes a kind of *phantom organ* emerge from the deconstructed piano; there is a fortissimo attack of a dense conglomerate of notes, a dissonant cluster, and it is in letting certain keys up that then start resonating, as if from a great distance, perfect major or minor chords, veritable *revenants* from a bygone era of harmony. The nostalgia for another world appears here for what it is: a revenant from a lost beyond, that it is a matter not of affirmatively grafting upon a restored faith, but literally of filtering through our fingers.

Lachenmann's opera, *The Little Match Girl*,[27] presents a gripping coda in which, after the death of the child, the otherworld of reconciliation resonates like a haunting ghost in the sonorities of a *shô*, the Japanese mouth organ. This work is in many ways the culmination of Lachenmann's long project on the corporeality of sound. The incredibly moving passages where the singers rub their chests in an evocation of the cold and of heating oneself up are taken up by the orchestra, the rubbing of the strings then giving birth to a surprising "instrumental concrete music," according to the composer's expression. There is no totalization here, no reconciliation or telharmonic fusion of bodies: What is given to be heard, *between* the material friction of bodies and the nostalgia (presented *as such*) of a perfect consonance from the other side of the grave, is the fragility of the gap.[28]

As I close this genealogy of musical bodies, I think of the *gamblers* Benjamin speaks of in his short story "The Lucky Hand," of those who gamble on a near or distant future by seeking in it "the hand-to-hand struggle with their fate." In their image, musical playing also often appears to me as "an artificially created danger." As Benjamin writes so well:

> In danger, it's true, the body reaches an understanding with things by passing above our brain. It's only once we are safe and sound that we understand what we have done. Our acts anticipated our knowledge. And if we condemn gambling, it is because it incites our organism to the most subtle and precise performances without any intervention from the mind.[29]

In the risk of musical body-to-body contact, the future, always, *is dispatched, pending* [*se dépêche en instance*].

P.S.

I was transported. Troubled, touched, moved above all, or in other words set into motion.

There was an accordionist, that morning in the metro. I had already been sitting down for several stations when he got in. He was probably expecting to start without delay once the train left. But first he waited a bit, like all the travelers, because of the "technical incident." Then, after a few minutes that must have seemed very long to him, standing in the middle of this stage without a stage, he certainly had to end up playing *Padam, Padam, Padam* . . . with a falsely confident air. But one sensed he was vexed by this untimely halt. His waltz rhythm seemed weak, as if it were bogged down. In his phrasing there was a kind of vexed movement, like the footsteps of someone setting their foot on a moving sidewalk that's not moving.

My body, like that of the other auditors that day, sitting down or standing up, seemed to grow heavy and numb, to sink.

But here we are in motion again. The train is already flying by at full speed. And although it's the same, the music is entirely different: It has become almost aerial, elastic. The three beats of its waltz are leaps and bounds. Things move forward. Contained smiles all around me. We are all transported.

I get off and change lines. No more musician this time but a river of thoughts and waking dreams.

I remember that marvelous scene that Kafka wrote down:

> The dancer Eduardova, a lover of music, travels in the tram, as everywhere else, in the company of two vigorous violinists whom she makes play often. For there is no known reason why one should not play in the tram if the playing is good, pleasing to the fellow passengers, and costs nothing; i.e., if the hat is not passed afterwards. Of course, at first it is a little surprising and for a short while everybody finds it improper. But at full speed, in a strong breeze and on a silent street, it sounds quite nice [*es klingt hübsch*].[1]

I tell myself that, in this experience that keeps recurring starting with the era of a certain movement in common of bodies, there is something like the setting into motion of musicality itself, through a transport that seizes and reveals it to those who find themselves carried away along with it.

This experience, apparently so close to that of bodies led by a conductor, is nonetheless very far from it. Here there is no common destination. At most, the fragile chance of going part of the way side by side.

NOTES

1. Interpreting Bodies

1. Friedrich Nietzsche, *Thus Spoke Zarathustra*, trans. Adrian Del Caro (Cambridge: Cambridge University Press, 2006), 23.
2. Franz Liszt, *An Artist's Journey: Lettres d'un bachelier ès musique, 1835–1841,* translated and annotated by Charles Suttoni (Chicago: University of Chicago Press, 1989), 45, emphasis mine.
3. Thomas Mace, *Musick's Monument*, facsimile edition (Paris: Editions du Centre national de la recherche scientifique, 1978), 33.
4. Thomas Bernhard, *The Loser: A Novel*, trans. Jack Dawson (New York: Vintage Books, 2006), 82.
5. Philippe Rousselot ("L'homme et l'instrument dans le répertoire libre," in *Instruments* [Paris: Ircam-Centre Pompidou, 1996]) cites more than one blues guitarist *introducing* his guitar in concert with a—generally feminine—first name: "Lucille," for example.
6. Letter from Gersdorff to Peter Gast, September 14, 1900, quoted by Georges Liébert, *Nietzsche and Music*, trans. David Pellauer and Graham Parkes (Chicago: University of Chicago Press, 2004), 20.
7. Peter Gast, quoted by Liébert, *Nietzsche and Music*, 204.
8. Friedrich Nietzsche, *Beyond Good and Evil*, trans. Walter Kaufmann (New York: Vintage, 1989), 24.
9. Collected in *The Will to Power*, trans. Walter Kaufmann and R. J. Hollingdale (New York: Vintage, 1967), 342. Even though I cannot give a rigorous explication of Nietzsche's thinking here, one must, nonetheless, in order to avoid its casual application (or its unscrupulous misappropriation), make several things clear. The cited

fragment actually states the following: "The will to power interprets (it is a question of interpretation when an organ is constructed): it defines limits, determines degrees, variations of power. . . . In fact, interpretation is itself a means of becoming master of something. (The organic process constantly presupposes interpretations.)" Heidegger has shown (in the first volume of his *Nietzsche*, trans. David Farrell Krell [New York: HarperOne, 1991], 33) that art was for Nietzsche "a configuration of the will to power, indeed, . . . its distinctive form." Now, this will to power can be understood, at least in part, as the exuberant affirmation of "life," displayed in particular in Dionysian "rapture" where music plays an essential role. Let us say then that "interpreting" in this context means: in the "rapture" of a musical body-to-body experience [*corps à corps*] that I am trying to analyze (and which has been for Nietzsche an exemplary "rapture" among other possible ones in art), in that state in which we "are . . . lifted beyond ourselves," we "embody" rather than "have" a body (as Heidegger admirably puts it, *Nietzsche*, 100).

2. Effictions

1. Denis Diderot, *Rameau's Nephew and d'Alembert's Dream*, trans Leonard Tancock (New York: Penguin, 1976), 103.
2. The figure was widely used in the medico-legal domain to identify a presumed criminal. Its poetic uses were codified by Geoffrey de Vinsauf in his *Poetria Nova* around 1200.
3. This is why we speak of sounds that are *high, low, shrill, piercing, deep, and heavy*; we say there is *friction* between two dissonant notes. . . . But when we say this, it is generally, or so we think, through figurative language, through metaphor, and thus in order to deny these bodies without body any *consistency*. Berlioz writes (*The Art of Music and Other Essays (À travers Chants)*, trans. Elizabeth Csicsery-Rónay [Bloomington: Indiana University Press, 1994], 21): "The words 'go up' or 'go down' are used to describe the movement of bodies that move away from the center of the earth or toward it. I challenge anyone to find another meaning for this pair of expressions. Now, how can sound, which is as imponderable as electricity or light, move away from or closer to the center of the earth by reason of its pitch? The words 'high' or 'sharp' are used to

describe the sound produced by a resonant body vibrating a certain number of times in a given length of time. A low or deep sound is the result of fewer vibrations in the same span, and therefore of slower vibrations. That is why the words 'slow' and 'grave' are more appropriate than 'low,' which indicates nothing to the purpose. Likewise a 'sharp' sound (which pierces the ear like a sharp object), *if taken figuratively* [emphasis mine], is a reasonable term, while a 'high' sound is absurd. For why should the sound produced by a string vibrating 32 times a second be closer to the center of the earth?" It is effectively reason itself that seems to dictate this protest (sounds do not have weight, therefore have no body), and that readily makes do with all kinds of analogies and comparisons to continue to hold that the world of music is hollowed out, empty of body and full of breath or soul. I am not speaking here of those *inspired* [*insufflés*] bodies (even if I think, unlike what Berlioz says, that they do weigh a certain weight). I am instead trying to grasp a process of becoming-body from before this detachment or flight, by which music breaks its ties to what makes it and to its hand-to-hand struggles, to cast off and become weightless as a way of closing itself up in an aerial world with its highs and lows and angles that at that point have become impalpable.

4. As Jean-Luc Nancy puts it in *Corpus*, trans. Richard Rand (New York: Fordham University Press, 2008).
5. Bernard Pautrat, in his fine essay on Nietzsche (*Versions du soleil. Figures et système de Nietzsche* [Paris: Seuil, 1971], 281) speaks of the "body's text." (Translation mine.—Trans.)
6. Diderot, *Rameau's Nephew and d'Alembert's Dream*, 156–57. Further page references in this chapter will be given parenthetically in the text.
7. See Johannes Lohmann, *Musiké und Logos: Aufsätze zur griechischen Philosophie und Musiktheorie* (Stuttgart: Musikwissenschaftliche Verlags-Gesellschaft, 1970).

3. Organologics (1): The Erasure of Bodies

1. That is, respectively, the harmony of the spheres or planets; the reflection of this celestial order in the human body, with its relation itself proportioned to the soul; and, finally, the more or less empty

category of an instrumental music that seems to be mentioned by Boethius only for rhetorical reasons. See Achim Diehr, *Speculum Corporis: Körpörlichkeit in der Musiktheorie des Mittelalters* (Kassel: Bärenreiter, 2000), 28–29.

2. Anicius Manlius Severinus Boethius, *Fundamentals of Music*, trans. Calvin M. Bower, Music Theory Translation Series, ed. Claude V. Palisca (New Haven: Yale University Press, 1989), 51.
3. Saint Augustine, *On Music*, trans. Robert Catesby Taliaferro, in vol. 2 of *The Fathers of the Church*, ed. Ludwig Schopp et al. (New York: Cima, 1947), 177: "Master. Now tell me, then, don't they all seem to be a kind with the nightingale, all those which sing well under the guidance of a certain sense, that is, do it harmoniously and sweetly, although if they were questioned about these numbers or intervals of high and low notes they could not reply? Disciple. I think they are very much alike. M. And what's more, aren't those who like to listen to them without this science to be compared to beasts? For we see elephants, bears, and many other kinds of beasts are moved by singing. . . . D. I judge so." And the disciple declares a bit further on: "And then explain, if you will, this great discipline which now can't seem to me so degraded as you make out" (187).
4. I can only refer here to Jean-Luc Nancy's wonderful pages in *Le Poids d'une pensée* (Grenoble: Griffon d'Aigle et Presses Universitaires de Grenoble, 1991) that should be put into dialogue with the following ironic statements from Erik Satie, so striking in relation to the musical fable from Pythagoras we are going to read: "Everyone will tell you I am not a musician. This is true. From the very beginning of my career, immediately I classed myself among the phonometricians. My work is pure phonometrics. . . . I get more pleasure from measuring a sound than I do from hearing it. With a phonometer in hand, I work joyfully and surely. What have I not weighed or measured? All of Beethoven, all Verdi, etc. It's very strange. The first time I used a phonoscope, I examined a B-flat of average size. I have never, I assure you, seen anything uglier. I called my servant in to show it to him. On the phono-scales an ordinary F-sharp, very common, reached 93 kilograms. It came from a strong, fat tenor whose weight I noted" (*Mémoires d'un amnésique: Ce que je suis*, cited by Anne Rey, *Satie* [Paris: Seuil, 1995], 13). (Translation mine.—Trans.)
5. Boethius, *Fundamentals*, 18–19.

6. Guido of Arezzo, *Micrologus*, in *Hucbald, Guido, and John on Music: Three Medieval Treatises*, trans. Warren Babb, Music Theory Translation Series 3, ed. Claude V. Palisca (New Haven: Yale University Press, 1978), 82.
7. Later on, the monochord, in strange circumstances, will be reproduced and metamorphosed in different keyboard instruments: starting in the thirteenth century, monochord, manicordion, manucordion, or polychord are equivalent names for instruments like the one described by Conrad von Zabern in his 1474 *Opusculum de monocordio*; and Johannes de Muris, in his 1323 *Musica speculativa*, was already speaking of a *monocordum* with nineteen strings [*sic*]. The monochord, that instrument that was meant to be purely theoretical, thus gave life to mechanized descendants equipped with keys. Striated, ruled, and divided into squares in black and white, these keyboards—ancestors of the piano—certainly continue to display the image of musical theory; they show scales, chords, keys, or intervals as different computable combinations in black and white. (Rousseau, in his 1767 *Dictionary of Music*, still gives as the first sense of "keyboard": "general stave [*portée*] or sum of the sounds of the entire system"; and it is only later that he mentions the current sense of "notes or keys.") Yet even as they keep their ancient function of theoretical exposition, these keyboards, as we will see, also expose knowledge to being touched by fingers without working through the logos of the musicus.
8. Boethius, *Fundamentals*, 19.
9. This monk's hand (reproduced in Smits van Waesberghe, *Musikerziehung, Lehre und Theorie der Musik im Mittelalter, Musikgeschichte in Bildern*, vol. 3, 3 [Leipzig: Deutscher Verlag für Musik, 1969]) is "read" from the initial *gamma* that designated G, the lowest note on the sound scale of medieval theoreticians (which gives the French word *gamme*, meaning scale).
10. Around 1470. The engraving is reproduced in Nigel Wilkins, *La Musique du diable* (Paris: Mardaga, 1999).

4. Touch-ups, or The Return of Bodies

1. Sebastian Virdung, *Musica getutscht: A Treatise on Musical Instruments*, ed. and trans. Beth Bullard (Cambridge: Cambridge University

Press, 1993), 115. Further page references to this work are given parenthetically in the text. It is true that Virdung seems to continue to diabolize percussion. About timpani, he writes, "They greatly disturb the peace of honourable, virtuous, old people; of the sick and ailing; of the religious in cloisters, who have to read, study, and pray." And he adds without hesitation, "I believe and consider it the truth [that] the devil invented and made them, for there is absolutely nothing pleasant or good about them. On the contrary, [they cause] a smothering and a drowning of all sweet melodies and of the whole of Music."

2. Epistle by Pseudo-Jerome, cited by Christian Meyer in his commentary on *Musica getutscht*, *Sebastian Virdung—Musica getuscht: Les instruments et la pratique musicale en Allemagne au début du XVIe siècle* (Paris: CNRS, 1980), 94–96. One of the first attested versions of the "Letter to Dardanus," in the ninth century, is found in Hrabanus Maurus, *De naturae rerum* (vol. 18, chap. 4). (Translation mine.—Trans.).
3. Denis Diderot, *Rameau's Nephew and d'Alembert's Dream*, trans. Leonard Tancock (New York: Penguin, 1976), 158.

5. Idiotisms, or The Dialect of Bodies

1. Sebastian Virdung, *Musica getutscht: A Treatise on Musical Instruments*, ed. and trans. Beth Bullard (Cambridge: Cambridge University Press, 1993), 99. Hereafter page references will be given parenthetically in the text.
2. The Littré dictionary recalls that in French, an *idiotisme* (from the Greek *idios*, proper, particular, special) is a construction or locution "proper and particular to a language."
3. The tablatures distinguish it from earlier works that described musical instruments, the two most important being the *Tractatus de Musica* by Paulirinius of Prague from around 1460 and the *De inventione et usu musicae* by Johannes Tinctoris from 1487. (See *Musica getutscht*, Christian Meyer's note, 21n40.) But among the three tablatures for organ, lute, and flute in the *Musica getutscht*, only the last two are properly digital. The one for organ is in effect absolutely similar to the first known tablature for keyboard (the Robertsbrige Codex from around 1320), which brings together two

forms of notation: the solfège (on staves) for the polyphony's upper voice, and letters to indicate the names of notes for the lower voices. It thus implies knowing how to *read* music: It is not unlinked from "song," in the sense Sebastian and Andreas give the word; it remains the result of knowledge, of a logos rising above particularities.

6. Monk, a Legend

1. Laurent De Wilde, *Monk*, trans. Jonathan Dickinson (New York: Marlow, 1997), 20.
2. Bill Evans, *A Statement*, in the book accompanying the CD *Conversations with Myself*, Polygram-Verve, recorded in 1963.
3. Jacques Ponzio and François Postif, *Blue Monk: Portrait de Thelonious* (Paris: Actes Sud, 1995), 31. (Translation mine.—Trans.)
4. De Wilde, *Monk*, 153.
5. Ibid.
6. Ibid., 152. See also Marc-Edouard Nabe, "Monk My Dear," *Le Jazzophone*, no. 15 (1983), cited in Ponzio and Postif, *Blue Monk*, 258: "He has two huge rings that bother him on each hand, and every time he hits three chords, he puts the ring back on; he turns it over, interrupts himself to do it, he does that every four chords he strikes; one of the hands arranges the other one and vice versa; it's as if he were screwing something in, as if he were screwing back in the huge fingers loosened by the music. . . . What if the fingers fell onto the keys? Actually, a pianist who puts rings like that on does so to get into his own way."
7. Ibid., 151. (Translation modified for completeness.—Trans.)
8. *The London Collection* (Black Lion). See Ponzio and Postif, *Blue Monk*, 357: "The sound engineer listens to the recording 1, then the recording 2, and shares his surprise: there is a strange percussion noise accompanying the music . . . the criminal body: Thelonius has excessively long nails and they hit the keys."
9. See Ponzio and Postif, *Blue Monk*, 259: "'To move heaven and earth' [*faire des pieds et des mains*, literally "to move hands and feet"] is not merely a figurative expression when one speaks of Thelonious. . . . According to the type of music being played, one can observe different steps. There is first of all a simple tempo marked

by the alternative pressure of the point and the heel. On *Nutty*, one can observe a variant on the famous play of the legs: the ice-skater's step. . . . Elsewhere, the sliding step of the cross-country skier alternates with the steps of the little rat in the Opera that marks syncopation." (Translation mine.—Trans.)

10. See chapters 13 and 14 for a fuller discussion of the term *autophony*.—Trans.

7. Traces of Fingers

1. Cf. Jean Haury, "Petite histoire illustrée de l'interface clavier," in *Les Nouveaux gestes de musique* (Paris: Editions Parenthèses, 1999), 93–94 (translation mine.—Trans.): "In 270 b.c., Ktesibios, a mechanic from Alexandria, invented the principle of the key and wind chest for a new musical instrument: the organ. For the first time, a mechanism is placed into an instrument to link a command, the key, to a sonorous body, the pipe. . . . Ktesibios creates the keyboard that arranges the pitches in an ascending order." Haury is referring to Hero of Alexandria's *Pneumatics* from the first century c.e. The sketch of the organist is reproduced by Haury from an eleventh-century manuscript. In his 1619 *De Organographia*, Michael Praetorius gives other engravings of ancient organ keyboards that are similar in every aspect.
2. See the article titled "Fingering" in the *New Grove Dictionary of Music and Musicians*.
3. François Couperin, *L'Art de toucher le clavecin (The Art of Playing the Harpsichord)*, ed. and trans. Margery Halford (Birmingham: Alfred, 1995).

8. Digital Rhetoric

1. The language and syntax of Couperin's treatise—like mine—sometimes suggest this parallel. Speaking of the fingers always implies a laborious and heavy-handed use of anaphora: this finger here, that one there, the first, the second, this last. In its syntactic gymnastics, the writing of treatises devoted to fingering painfully reflects the contortions of the hand.

2. César Chesneau Du Marsais, *Des Tropes* (Paris: Jean-Baptiste Broca, 1730), 8–9. (Translation mine.—Trans.)
3. Ibid., 14–15. (Translation mine.—Trans.)

9. Ablations and Grafts (Too Many Fingers)

1. Carl Philipp Emanuel Bach, *Versuch über die wahre Art das Clavier zu spielen mit Exempeln und achtzehn Probe-Stücken in sechs Sonaten* (Berlin, 1753; facsimile reproduction, Bärenreiter, 1994). See also the English translation by William J. Mitchell: *Essay on the True Art of Playing Keyboard Instruments* (Eulenberg, 1974). (I have modified Mitchell's translations.—Trans.)
2. Carl Philipp Emmanuel Bach, "Von der Finger-Setzung," in *Versuch über die wahre Art*, §1.
3. The *a contrario* proof of this is that on some old recorder flutes, for the ring finger that would find itself on the bottom of the tube, the interchangeability of the hands demanded that a double hole be pierced: one of the holes shifted to the left and the other to the right (as can be seen on one of the engravings illustrating Virdung's *Musica getutscht* reproduced above in chapter 5.) This shows that the positions of the musical body are, unlike the keyboard, largely preconstructed or prefabricated *in* the instrumental body. At least as long as one is playing in an "orthodox" way—and this is the only reason why in this case, provisionally, we are privileging keyboards.
4. Bach, "Von der Finger-Setzung," §6.
5. Ibid., §13, emphasis mine.
6. Ibid., §2.

10. Romantic Fingers (System of Touch)

1. François-Joseph Fétis, *Méthode des méthodes de piano* (Paris, 1840). Further references to sections of this book are given within parentheses in the text. (Translations mine.—Trans.)
2. Ibid., chap. 3: "On Tact, or The Way of Hitting the Keys," 8–10, emphasis mine. (Translation mine.—Trans.)
3. It may at first seem surprising to affirm that the Romantic era for the keyboard is that of the standardization of how it is played. If, in

the manufacture of pianos, this normalization is attested and acknowledged (constructing and selling pianos becomes an industry), we have a tendency to represent the golden age of virtuosi (Liszt, Chopin . . .) as comprising a landscape of exacerbated individualities. There is, however, I think, no contradiction here: The individuation of musical passions (whose pre-Romantic premises are in fact found in Carl Philipp Emmanuel Bach's writing, which describes the musician as "constantly changing passion"), the singularization and mobility of the affects, supposes, as its obverse or reverse, the implosion of every hierarchized system (of every *Affektenlehre* and *Figurenlehre*) and, because of this, the basis for an egalitarian digital rhetoric that correlatively gives values to the individual (virtuosic) *deviations*. This is what one clearly understands from one passage of the *Method of Methods*, where the normed and regular playing of the "schools" is increasingly placed in opposition to the differences of those individualities whose prime examples are Liszt and Thalberg: "The linked, equal and polished playing of the Clementi and Kalkbrenner schools is remarkable in the high degree of correction of the mechanism and its elegant easiness. Everything is beautiful, pure, and *regular* in the types of these schools. . . . [To the contrary], Liszt's playing . . . is *the greatest imaginable deviation one can imagine from the school* of Hummel. The delicateness of touch is not the main object of his talent, and his attention goes to the increase in the piano's strength, and to the necessity of bringing this strength closer to the orchestra's, as much as is possible. Whence *certain combinations that are particular to him* in the frequent recourse to the pedals with special procedures for hitting the keys; combinations that are very impressive but that demand long and in-depth study of the instrument as well as lots of nervous strength. Mr. Thalberg's attention is also drawn to the increase of the piano's strength, and it's in the realization of these considerations that his admirable talent developed; but in order to reach the goal he set for himself, his ways of proceeding were different from Liszt's. Considering that piano music, by acquiring its brilliancy, brought the right hand to high notes, while the left hand hits the low notes, and since as a result of this disposition, the middle of the keyboard often remains unoccupied, and leaves a void in the harmony, he decided to throw a singing part with sustained sounds into the middle while a brilliant part would make itself heard in the high sounds, accompanied by a powerful bass. He resolved this difficult problem in the happiest of ways, and *his playing offers the strange illusion of a keyboard occupied by three or four nimble hands*" (Fétis, *Méthode des méthodes*, §§9–10, emphasis mine).

4. I list these remarkable "figures" in no order and without mentioning the most frequent ones: "the progressive repetition of the same fingering on the same series of [notes]," the "passage of the thumb under the other fingers and of the other fingers over the thumb," the "extensions" and "leaps," "the use of the thumb and of the fifth finger on the black keys," the "passage of one finger over another, shorter one" or the "passage of one finger under another, longer one," the "alternating use of several fingers on only one key while holding or repeating the note." As for the "freedoms" or "exceptions," these are, still in rhetorical terms, either *catachresis*, in other words obligated figures because there is no possible "normal" choice (§107: "the exceptional fingering is the one in which certain combinations of the music make it necessary to not make use of the easy and regular means"), or artifices of expression. (See §79: "The change of a finger on a non-repeated note is the most rarely used fingering artifice and the one that demands the most dexterity in order to execute it . . . Kalkbrenner recommends its frequent use [. . .] because, he says, the major defect of the piano being that it is dry when it is played poorly, through all means possible one must seek to avoid raising the fingers too much, and to tie the notes together as much as is possible." As we can see, the relays of fingers on one and the same key, recommended by Couperin in order to link [*lier*] better, have become the licentious deviations reserved to the greatest virtuosi.) In this standardized digital landscape, only Chopin seems to provide an exception, at least to judge by his teaching. Concerning his "Art of fingering," he is not far from thus proposing what we might call an *ecology of fingering*: "The goal isn't to learn to play everything with an equal sound. A well-formed technique, it seems to me, [is one] that can control and vary [*bien nuancer*] a beautiful sound quality. For a long time we have been acting against nature by training our fingers to be all equally powerful. As each finger is differently formed, it's better not to attempt to destroy the particular charm of each one's touch but on the contrary to develop it. Each

finger's power is determined by its shape. The thumb has the most power, being the broadest, shortest, and freest; the fifth [finger] as the other extremity of the hand; the third as the middle and the pivot; then the second [. . .], and then the fourth, the weakest one, the Siamese twin of the third, bound to it by a common ligament, and which people insist on trying to separate—which is impossible and, fortunately, unnecessary. As many sounds as there are fingers—everything is a matter of knowing good fingering. . . . Just as we need to use the conformation of the fingers, we need no less to use the rest of the hand, the wrist, the forearm and the arm" (Jean-Jacques Eigeldinger, *Chopin: Pianist and Teacher as Seen by His Pupils,* trans. Naomi Shohet with Krysia Osostowicz and Roy Howat [Cambridge: Cambridge University Press, 1986], 195).

11. Feet

1. According to the same principle, clavichords with pedals have existed since the fifteenth century, as have, starting in the eighteenth, harpsichords or pianos with pedals: Mozart had one made for him in 1785, and Schumann devoted his *Etudes* opus 56 to it.
2. Charles Chaulieu, "Des pédales du piano et d'un signe nouveau," in *Le Pianiste*, no. 9, (Paris, 1833–34), 131–32. (Translation mine.—Trans.)
3. The literal translation for the expression Szendy uses here is *to take one's foot*.—Trans.
4. See David Rowland, *A History of Pianoforte Pedalling* (Cambridge: Cambridge University Press, 1993).

12. Joyful Tropiques (Evolution, Revolutions)

1. François Couperin, *L'Art de toucher le clavecin (The Art of Playing the Harpsichord),* ed. and trans. Margery Halford (Birmingham: Alfred, 1995), 33.
2. Carl Philipp Emanuel Bach, *Von den Vorschlagen,* in *Versuch über die wahre Art das Clavier zu spielen mit Exempeln und achtzehn Probe-Stücken in sechs Sonaten* (Berlin, 1753; facsimile reproduction, Bärenreiter, 1994), §1; several pages further on, the mordant is also qualified as "a necessary ornament that ties the notes to one another."

3. Carl Philipp Emanuel Bach, *Vom Vortrage*, ibid., §7.
4. One would in particular have to add a whole host of other *pedagogical* prostheses—all equally necessary to the formation, deformation, and reformation of the keyboardist's body—whose nomenclature was sketched out by Couperin in the following terms: "To mold and form the hands by exercises at the harpsichord, . . . one must begin with the position of the body. In order to be seated at the correct height, the under side of the elbows, wrists and the fingers must be all on one level: so one must choose *a chair* which agrees with this rule. It will be necessary to put *something of suitable height* under young people's feet, measured by their growth, so that their feet are not dangling in the air and so they can keep their bodies properly balanced. If a person has too high a wrist in playing, the only remedy I have found is to have someone hold *a little flexible stick* which is passed over the faulty wrist" (Couperin, *Art of Playing the Harpsichord*, 29, emphasis mine). And so on.
5. *E. T. A. Hoffmann's Musical Writings*, ed. David Charlton, trans. Martyn Clarke (Cambridge: Cambridge University Press, 1989), 140.

13. *Two Dispatches (One Fictive and the Other Dreamed Up)*

1. Ferruccio Busoni, "A Fairy-Like Invention," in *The Essence of Music and Other Papers*, translated from the German by Rosamond Ley (New York: Dover, 1965), 190–93.
2. Pure writing then? The phonograph record, Adorno said in a wonderful little text from 1934, "re-establishes . . . an age-old, submerged and yet warranted relationship: that between music and *writing*" ("Die Form der Schallplatte," reprinted in *Musikalische Schriften VI* (*Gesammelte Schriften*, vol. 19 [Frankfurt: Suhrkamp, 1984], 530–34; English translation by Thomas Y. Levin, *October* 55 [Winter 1990]: 59). Had Adorno received and read Aprilus's despatch? Whatever the case may be, the writing [*Schrift*] Adorno speaks of has nothing "historical" about it; it has nothing to do with, for example, the Western and dated invention of solmization or of notation on staff: With the record, he says, "music, previously conveyed by writing, suddenly turns itself into writing." It is thus rather something of a cypher, of a tracing that would have pertained to music since a

properly immemorial time. From a past older than any memory, which also opens onto the extreme point of the future, onto a day that would be something like the last day: When music turns itself into phono-graphic writing, adds Adorno citing Benjamin, it is "with the hope that, once fixed in this way, it will some day become readable as the 'last remaining universal language since the construction of the tower of Babel,' a language whose determined yet encrypted expressions are contained in each of its 'phrases.'"

3. Novalis, *Philosophical Writings*, trans. and ed. Margaret Mahony Stoljar (Albany: State University of New York Press, 1997), 153.
4. Marin Mersenne, *Harmonie universelle* (1636), book 7, "On Percussion Instruments," proposition 1. (Translation mine.—Trans.)
5. Ibid., book 1, prop. 1.

14. *Organologics (2): Autophony*

1. André Schaeffner, *Origine des instruments de musique* (1968; reedited, Paris: Ecole des Hautes études en sciences sociales, 1994), 102, 108. (Translation mine.—Trans.)
2. Ibid.
3. A deconstruction of organology, which remains yet to be done, and which I am partially attempting here, should take into account the path broken by Bernard Stiegler in his critique of anthropology (see *Technics and Time*, vol. 1, *The Fault of Epimetheus*, trans. Richard Beardsworth and George Collins [Stanford, Calif.: Stanford University Press, 1998]).
4. Curt Sachs, *Reallexikon der Musikinstrumente* (Hildesheim: Georg Olms Verlag, 1979), 195.
5. Curt Sachs and Erich von Hornbostel, "Systematik der Musikinstrumente," *Zeitschrift für Ethnologie* (Berlin, 1914).
6. Schaeffner, *Origine des instruments de musique*, 143–44. (Translation mine.—Trans.)

15. *Genesis (1): Ocular Harpsichord, Organ of Flavors*

1. Other than its brief and discrete passage in *D'Alembert's Dream*, this ocular harpsichord notably appears in the article "Animal" of the

Encyclopedia, in the "Letter on the Blind" and in a letter to Madame de Maux (in which Diderot writes, "Well, my friend, that instrument is me" (Denis Diderot, *Oeuvres complètes* [Paris: Le Club français du livre, 1973], 7:953)).

2. Denis Diderot, "Extraits de l'*Encyclopédie*," in *Oeuvres complètes*, 15:190.
3. We find it mentioned by Rousseau (*Essay on the Origin of Languages*), Georg Philipp Telemann (*Beschreibung der Augen-Orgel oder Augen-Clavicimbels. . .*, 1739), and by many others.
4. Castel, "Clavecin pour les yeux," in *Esprits, saillies et singularités du père Castel*, pieces chosen and gathered by Joseph de La Porte, 1763, 280. (Translation mine.—Trans.)
5. I will not resist the pleasure of citing the rest of this passage: ". . . tastes . . . have, like sonorous bodies, their generative tones, dominants, majors, minors, low- and high-pitched . . . & everything that depends on them, as a result their consonances and their dissonances. Seven full tones are the fundamental basis for sound Music: the same number of primitive tastes are the basis for flavorful Music, & their harmonic combination is made with similar reasoning. [There then follows a staff where one can read the following correspondences: *do* is "acidic," *re* is "bland," *mi* is "sweet," *fa* is "bitter," *sol* is "sweet and sour," *la* is "austere," *si* is "spicy."] . . . mix Acid with Sweet and Sour, . . . Lemon, for example, with sugar, and you will have a simple yet charming consonance, in fifths. . . . The Dissonances are not less analogous in one & the other Music . . . in flavorful Music, mix Acid with Bitter: Vinegar, for example, with Absynth, the composite will be despicable."
6. *Esprit, saillies et singularités de P. Castel*, 369. This general organology of the senses, as one sees, is much earlier than the famous *A Rebours* by Huysmans, where des Esseintes calls his collection of "barrels of liquors" a "mouth organ" (chap. 4): On this keyboard where each liquor corresponds "to the sound of an instrument"—"dry curaçao, for example, to the clarinet whose song is slightly bitter and velvety"—des Esseintes "was able to obtain . . . sensations analogous to those that music gives to the ear."
7. On the history of synesthesia, see my "Toucher à soi (C., ou le clavecin des sens)," *Les Cahiers du Musée national d'art moderne*, no.

74 (2001). It remains to be seen why, in this fabulous genealogy, harpsichords occupy stage front. The Doctor Bordeu to whom Diderot gives voice suggests at least one hypothesis, that of a certain primacy of touch, one that Jacques Derrida proposed that we name "haptocentrism" (see *On Touching—Jean-Luc Nancy*, trans. Christine Irizarry (Stanford, Calif.: Stanford University Press, 2005)). Bordeu does indeed declare that "this pure and simple sensitivity, this sense of touch, is differentiated through the organs that arise from each separate fiber; one fiber, forming an ear, gives rise to *a kind of touch* that we call noise or sound; another forming the palate, gives rise to *a second kind of touch* that we call taste . . ." Etc. (*Rameau's Nephew and D'Alembert's Dream*, trans. Leonard Tancock [New York: Penguin, 1976], 108–9).

8. Athanasius Kircher, *Musurgia universalis*, book 10, part 1, chapter 1, "Deus Opt. Max. Organaedo, Mundus organo comparator" (Rome, 1650), 365–67. (Translation mine.—Trans.)
9. *Arnold Schoenberg Letters*, ed. Erwin Stein, trans. Eithne Wilkins and Ernst Kaiser (New York: Saint Martin's Press, 1965), 54.

16. Telepathy

1. Denis Diderot, *Rameau's Nephew and d'Alembert's Dream*, trans Leonard Tancock (New York: Penguin, 1976), 189.
2. Marie Jaëll (1846–1925), a child prodigy and virtuoso, student of Moschelès, spouse of the pianist Alfred Jaëll, friend and secretary to Liszt in 1883 (who nicknamed her *Ossiana*, based on her symphonic poem with that title), left one didactic work: *Les Rythmes du regard et la dissociation des doigts* [The rhythms of the gaze and the dissociation of fingers] (Paris: Librairie Fischbacher, 1906). The excerpts that follow from her *Cahiers de travail* [Exercise notebooks] and *Un nouvel état de conscience* [A new state of consciousness] (Alcan, 1910) are cited in Hélène Kiener, *Marie Jaëll: Problèmes d'esthétique et de pédagogie musicales* [Problems in musical aesthetics and pedagogy] (Paris: Flammarion, 1952). (Translation mine.—Trans.)
3. Jaëll, *Cahiers.*
4. Jaëll, *Les Rythmes du regard.*

5. Sigmund Freud, *New Introductory Lectures on Psycho-Analysis*, trans. James Strachey, (New York: Norton [Standard Edition]), 1990), 44–45, emphasis mine.
6. Ibid., 68.
7. See Jacques Derrida, "Telepathy," trans. Nicholas Royle, in *Psyché: Inventions of the Other*, ed. Peggy Kamuf and Elizabeth Rottenberg (Stanford, Calif.: Stanford University Press, 2007), 1:226–61.
8. *Telepathy* is a word that appeared at the end of the nineteenth century (1882, according to the *Oxford English Dictionary*) and was forged by a certain Frederic Myers, who proposes it as an equivalent for *telesthesia* in order to "cover all cases of impression received at a distance without the normal operation of the recognized sense organs" (statements by Myers during a meeting of the Society for Physical Research in London in December 1882). For further details see Nicholas Royle's fine study, *Telepathy and Literature: Essays on the Reading Mind* (London: Basil Blackwell, 1990).
9. Walter Benjamin, "Telepathie" (1927–28), in *Gesammelte Schriften*, ed. Rolf Tiedemann and Hermann Schweppenhäuser (Frankfurt am Main: Suhrkamp, 1985), 6:187–88. (Translation mine.—Trans.)
10. Walter Benjamin, *Selected Writings*, ed. Michael Jennings, Howard Eiland, and Gary Smith (Cambridge, Mass.: Harvard University Press, 2005), 2:297.
11. Ibid., 298, emphasis mine.

17. Scruples (Clones and Stand-ins)

1. Denis Diderot, *Rameau's Nephew and d'Alembert's Dream*, trans. Leonard Tancock (New York: Penguin, 1976), 172. Page numbers for subsequent references are given parenthetically in the text.
2. Walter Benjamin speaks of the "highly developed shame feeling among children": "That they so frequently feel shame," he writes, "is connected with the fact that they have so much fantasy, particularly in their earliest maturity" ("Erröten in Zorn und Scham," in Gesammelte Schriften, ed. Rolf Tiedemann and Hermann Schweppenhäuser, 6:120 [Translation mine.—Trans.]).

3. "Kind und Pferd—Kentaur," in Gesammelte Schriften, ed. Rolf Tiedemann and Hermann Schweppenhäuser, 6:191–92. (Translation mine.—Trans.)

18. Conducting (Seen from the Back)

1. "Kind und Pferd—Kentaur," in Gesammelte Schriften, ed. Rolf Tiedemann and Hermann Schweppenhäuser, 6:191–92.
2. Elias Canetti, "The Orchestral Conductor," in *Crowds and Power*, trans. Carol Stewart (New York: Farrar, Straus and Giroux, 1984), 394–96, emphasis mine.
3. *Le Chef d'orchestre: Théorie de son art*, first published as an appendix to the English-language edition of his *Traité d'instrumentation*. Georges Liébert included this text, with many other treatises on orchestra direction, in a collection titled *L'Art du chef d'orchestre* (Paris: Hachette, coll. "Pluriel," 1988). (Today in French the *conducteur* is referred to, as these titles show, as a *chef d'orchestre*.—Trans.)
4. Theodor Adorno, *Introduction to the Sociology of Music*, trans. E. B. Ashton (New York: Seabury Press, 1976), 105. (Translation modified.—Trans.)
5. Ibid., 104.
6. See the article "Cheironomy," in the *New Grove Dictionary of Music and Musicians*.

19. Genesis (2): **Fantasia,** *or "Plasmaticity"*

1. Sergei Eisenstein, *Disney*, ed. Oskana Bulgakowa and Dietmar Hochmuth, trans. Dustin Condres (Berlin: Potemkin Press, 2011), 33.
2. *Magic of Art*, cited in Eisenstein, *Walt Disney*, ed. Naum Kleiman (Paris: Circé, 1991), 118n32.
3. Cited by John Culhane, *Walt Disney's Fantasia* (New York: Abradale Press, 1999), 36.
4. Cited in Culhane, *Fantasia*, 38.
5. "Cinema en relief," cited in *Walt Disney*, ed. Naum Kleiman (Paris: Circé, 1991), 114n17.

20. Touching from Afar

1. Nietzsche stated this in the following terms in *Daybreak*, trans. R. J. Hollingdale (Cambridge: Cambridge University Press, 1997), §307, p. 156: "*Facta! Yes, Facta ficta!*—A historian has to do, not with what actually happened, but only with events supposed to have happened: for only the latter have *produced an effect*. . . . His theme, so-called world history, is opinions about supposed actions and their supposed motives, which in turn give rise to further opinions and actions, the reality of which is however at once vaporized again and produces an *effect* only as vapour—a continual generation and pregnancy of phantoms over the impenetrable mist of unfathomable reality. All historians speak of things which have never existed except in imagination."
2. See in particular Plato, *Apology of Socrates*, 26e and Aristotle, *Problems*, 901b30; on Greek theater as trance, see Gilbert Rouget, *Music and Trance*, translation from the French revised by Bruhilde Biebuyck in collaboration with the author (Chicago: University of Chicago Press, 1985).
3. See the article "Orchester," in *Die Musik in Geschichte und Gegenwart* (Kassel: Bärenreiter and Metzler, 1994–2007).
4. Jean-Jacques Rousseau, *A Complete Dictionary of Music*, trans. William Waring (London: J. Murray, 1779), 301–2.
5. Carl Philipp Emanuel Bach to Forkel, quoted in Martin Geck, *Johann Sebastian Bach: Life and Work*, translated from the German by John Hargraves (New York: Harcourt Books, 2006), 77–78.
6. Quoted in *The New Bach Reader: A Life of Johann Sebastian Bach in Letters and Documents*, edited by Hans T. David and Arthur Mendel, revised and expanded by Christoph Wolff (New York: Norton Paperback, 1998), 328–29.
7. F. W. von Grimm, "The Little Prophet of Boehmischbroda" (1753), in *Source Readings in Music History. From Classical Antiquity through the Romantic Era*, selected and annotated by Oliver Strunk (New York: Norton, New York, 1950), 623.
8. André Ernest Modeste Grétry, *Mémoires, ou Essais sur la musique* (Paris: Imprimerie de la République, 1796), 39–40. (Translation mine.—Trans.)
9. Ibid., 41–42.

10. Charles Burney, *An Account of the Musical Performances in Westminster Abbey and the Pantheon, May 26th, 27th, 29th; and June the 3rd and 5th, 1784* (London, 1785).
11. On an 1843 concert tour in Germany, Berlioz will thus exchange his "heavy piece of oak" for the light baton of Mendelssohn (who had taken the direction of the orchestra of the Gewandhaus of Leipzig in 1835). This exchange seals their friendship as conductors in the lexicon of war, the kind that children play; on February 2, 1843, Berlioz writes to Mendelssohn: "Great Chief! We are pledged to exchange tomahawks. Here is mine. It is rough-hewn. Yours is plain. . . . Be my brother, and when the Great Spirit sends us to hunt in the land of souls, may our warriors hang our tomahawks side by side at the door of the council-chamber." Cited in Carlton Hughes, *Moments for Music* (Lincoln, Neb.: Writers Club Press, 2002), 30.
12. Hector Berlioz, "The Conductor and His Art," in Hugh Macdonald, *Berlioz's Orchestration Treatise: A Translation and Commentary* (Cambridge: Cambridge University Press, 2004), 353–55.
13. Ibid., 337. (Translation slightly modified.—Trans.)
14. Cited in Georges Liébert, *L'Art du chef d'orchestre* (Paris: Hachette, 1988), 56.
15. Charles Burney, *An Account of the Musical Performances in Westminster Abbey*, 15.
16. Hector Berlioz, "Euphonia, or the Musical City," in *Evenings with the Orchestra*, trans. and ed. Jacques Barzun (Chicago: University of Chicago Press, 1956), 286–87.
17. In *Die Musik in Geschichte und Gegenwart*, under the article "Orchester," Helmut Rösing writes: "In the eighteenth century, lists of orchestra members were often printed, the main musicians and their remarkable talents were named, biographical elements about them were indicated, in short, the orchestra was seen as a group of singular interpreters, of which the majority could in fact often be employed as soloists. On the contrary, in the nineteenth century, the orchestra was increasingly posed as a totality faced with the individual, with the virtuoso. It was conceived of as a collective whose members were mostly anonymous."
18. Gabriel Tarde, *The Laws of Imitation,* translated by Elsie C. Parsons (New York: Henry Holt, 1903; reprinted by BiblioBazaar, 2009), 134. (Translation modified for completeness.—Trans.)

19. Cited by Georges Liébert, *L'Art du chef d'orchestre*, 66. (Translation mine.—Trans.)

20. Theodor Adorno, *Introduction to the Sociology of Music*, trans. E. B. Ashton (New York: Seabury Press, 1976), 110. (Translation modified.—Trans.) In 1909, Camille Mauclair, in *La religion de la musique*, gathered into one extended metaphor the images of the trainer, despot, magnetizer, lightning-conductor, etc., all the way through the conductor communicating with the divine: "This man plays directly on the nerves of two thousand other creatures with as much sureness as a voltaic thread making a muscle tremble. And sometimes he conjures and at others he calls out, struggles, unleashes, calms, protests, reassures, or frightens his people, and makes a sudden gesture of silence, as if begging, with caressing hands, the Being not to emerge from its shadow." Cited by Georges Liébert, *L'Art du chef d'orchestre*, 113–14. (Translation mine.—Trans.)

21. Organologics (3): Areality

1. Jean-Luc Nancy, *Corpus*, trans. Richard Rand (New York: Fordham University Press, 2008), 43.

2. André Schaeffner, *Origine des instruments de musique* (1968; Paris: Ecole des hautes études en sciences sociales, 1994).

3. For Schaeffner, this dispossession can be sensed very early in the chain: "The transfer of the properly sonorous action to the extremity of a handle" is already described as a "complication of the technical apparatus" that "takes extremely precious possibilities of contact, of *touching* away from the hand" (ibid., 58).

4. In Béla Bartók's "Mechanical Music," in *Essays*, selected and edited by Benjamin Suchoff (London: Faber and Faber, 1976), 290 (written in 1937), this break is truly obsessive, in the insistence of the adverb "already" (emphasis mine): "There is *already* no control of the sound of plucked instruments other than the moment when the vibration is initiated. The same is true of string instruments with levers, such as the piano. There are certain plucked instruments whose strings can be shortened with the fingers, but on the harp or the piano, for instance, this kind of direct connection between vibrating and human bodies is *already* not possible. The piano string, moreover, is vibrated by means of mechanically produced

energy transfer. In reality, therefore, we could *already* designate piano music as a more or less mechanized music." (Translation modified for accuracy.—Trans.) This text by Bartók (and this *already*, whose anxious scansion I analyzed in *Musica practica* [Paris: Harmattan, 1997]) perhaps testifies better than anything else to the fact that the continuist perspective is haunted by the nature versus technique opposition that it seeks to postpone: The split is constantly returning, resurging, *already*, *already*.

22. Bodies Electric

1. François-Joseph Fétis, "Diviss or Diwisch," in *Biographie universelle des musiciens* (Paris, 1874). (Translation mine.—Trans.) See also the article "Denis d'or" (by Hugh Davies) in the *New Grove Dictionary of Musical Instruments*: "A keyboard instrument developed by Prokop Diviš . . . from about 1730, and finally completed in 1762. Diviš . . . carried out research into the properties of static electricity and devised, among other things, a lightning conductor in 1754 (anticipating Benjamin Franklin's invention by six years). The *Denis d'or* . . . was the first musical instrument to involve electricity, though this was probably not an essential part of its action: Diviš claimed that the performer could be given an electric shock 'as often as the inventor wished.'"
2. See Jean-Baptiste Delaborde, *Les Lettres sur le Clavessin électrique*, in *Le Clavessin électrique, avec une nouvelle théorie du méchanisme et des phénomènes de l'électricité: Par le R. P. Delaborde, de la Compagnie de Jésus* (Paris : Chez H. L. Guerin and L. F. Delatour, 1761; Geneva: Minkoff Reprint, 1997), 1–2, emphasis mine. (Translation mine.—Trans.)
3. If the proportions of an organ's pipes are determined by the pitch of the notes to be produced, its air or water machinery is certainly not; but it is not as extensible in space as an electrical cord.
4. Here again, if the idea of a "composite" instrument does not date from electricity (the "organized" harpsichord, already in existence at the start of the sixteenth century, would be a good example, with its organ pipes coupled with strings and set into action by the keys of a harpsichord), it is the distance between the components that

electricity allows that turns the instrument into a veritable network, in other words a reticulated space.

5. See Reynold Weidenaar, *Magic Music from the Telharmonium* (Lanham, Md.: Scarecrow Press, 1995), from whom I am taking most of the following documents. Weidenaar writes: "Astonishingly, music transmitted over wires is older than the telephone itself. As early as 1851, . . . Edward Farrar began experimenting with a fledgling musical telegraph. He devised a reed melodeon for sending tones over telegraph lines to an electromagnetic receiver" (1).
6. See ibid., 2, which cites "Music by Telegraph," *New York Times*, July 10, 1874.
7. According to an April 3, 1877 account in the *New York Times* (cited by Weidenaar, *Magic Music from the Telharmonium*, 2), this music "as a novelty, was highly entertaining, though unless an almost incredible improvement be effected, it is difficult to see how the transmission of music over the new instrument can be of permanent practical value."
8. See Weidenaar, *Magic Music from the Telharmonium*, 3–4; it seems that the "smuggler" in the matter of these "telemusical" technologies was a certain Theodor Puskás, who collaborated with Edison starting in 1875, before moving to Paris and later to Budapest.
9. Ibid., 28. "U.S. Patent 580,035, Art of and Apparatus for Generating and Distributing Music Electrically, Thaddeus Cahill, New York, patented April 6, 1897."
10. According to Jean-Claude Risset's expression ("Synthèse et matériau musical," in *Cahiers de l'Ircam*, no. 2, 1993).
11. "Music on Wires," *New York Globe and Commercial Advertiser*, January 31, 1907, cited in Weidenaar, 136.
12. See Georges Sbriglia, *L'Exploitation des oeuvres musicales par les instruments de musique mécaniques et le droit de l'auteur* (Paris: Arthur Rousseau Editeur, 1907).
13. See my *Listen: A History of the Ears*, trans. Charlotte Mandel (New York: Fordham University Press, 2008).
14. Cited in Weidenaar, *Magic Music from the Telharmonium*,177, emphasis mine.
15. Cited by Joachim Stange, *Die Bedeutung der elektroakustischen Medien für die Musik im 20. Jahrhundert* (Herboltsheim: Centaurus-Verlag, 1989), 128, emphasis mine.

16. Cited in Marc Battier, "L'approche gestuelle dans l'histoire de la lutherie électronique: Etude de cas: Le Theremin," in *Les Nouveaux gestes de la musique*, 142, emphasis mine. (Translation mine.—Trans.)
17. Cited in Stange, *Die Bedeutung*, 129.
18. Cited ibid., 132, emphasis mine.

23. Mass Formations

1. Achim Diehr (*Speculum Corporis*, esp. 56–57) shows how the medieval idea of the universe forming a song (*universum esse velut canticum. . .*, as Guillaume d'Auvergne writes in his *De anima*, V, 18) refers to a general "contexture" (*contextio*) that interweaves the macrocosm of celestial bodies and the microcosm of the membered human body. In other words, between the hand and the forearm, between the forearm and the arm, etc., a harmony must exist that is analogous to the one that organizes the proportions of distance between the planets.
2. In a posthumous fragment from 1885, Nietzsche described the "human body" (in other words what Zarathustra calls the "self") as "an immense gathering of living beings, all dependent and subordinate, but in another sense dominant and active according to their own will" (cited and commented on by Barbara Siegler in her remarkable work *Nietzsche et la biologie* [Paris: Presses Universitaires de France, 2001], 25). This Nietzschean "metaphor," which he borrows from the biology of his time (and which is perhaps a catachresis, an obligatory figure or a necessary ornament, so true is it that the body could not be "properly" stated without recourse to the "images" of a collective), is also found, insistent, in the time's sociology. See, for example, in Gustave Le Bon (*The Crowd: A Study of the Popular Mind*, 1895, cited in fact by Freud): "The psychological crowd is a provisional being formed of heterogeneous elements, which for a moment are combined, exactly as the cells which constitute a living body."
3. This is the "133rd year" of this "symphony" (reproduced in Nam June Paik, *Du Cheval à Christo et autres écrits* [Paris: Editions Lebeer Hossmann, 1993], 190). (Translation mine.—Trans.) Already in 1961, one finds a similarly telharmonic project, though one limited to "earthly" space (Paik, *Du Cheval*, 229): "In San Francisco playing

the left hand of fugue no. 1 (C major) from 'well-tempered 1' (J. S. Bach) / In Shanghai playing the right hand of fugue no. 1 (C major) from 'well-tempered 1' (J. S. Bach) / Begin exactly at 12:00 . . .—this can be simultaneously diffused on both sides of the ocean." Stockhausen is often mentioned in Paik's writing, particularly in *The Exposition of Music*, which appeared in 1962.

4. Stockhausen describes the apparatus of *Helikopter-Streichquartett* (1991–92, but the premiere did not take place until 1995 in Amsterdam) in the following way: string quartet, four helicopters (flying at a high altitude in a perimeter of about six kilometers) with pilots and four sound engineers, four video transmitters, four audio transmitters, an auditorium with four columns of television screens and four columns of loudspeakers, a "sound projectionist" with a mixing console (see www.stockhausen.org). The project of this work, he says, was first glimpsed in a dream: "I heard and saw the four string players in four helicopters flying in the air and playing. . . . Most of the time, the[y] played tremoli which blended so well with the timbres and the rhythms of the rotor blades that the helicopters sounded like musical instruments. When I woke up, I strongly felt that something had been communicated to me." To realize this sound fusion in which the string instruments must slightly dominate, Stockhausen suggests using transmitters linked together by satellite, capable of being simultaneously received in the auditorium and in other eventual places. *Helikopter-Streichquartett* is the third scene of the third day of the opera *Licht*; it is "dedicated to all astronauts."

5. As he wrote in 1971 about *Sternklang* ("Stellar Sound"), for five groups of singers and instrumentalists separated from one another in the space of a park (see his *Texte*, 4:172–74). Must we inscribe into this lineage, as its ultimate development, Stockhausen's recent statements about the September 11, 2001, attacks, which he described as "the biggest work of art there has ever been"? Must these sentences (pronounced during a press conference in Hamburg on September 16, 2001, and integrally transcribed since then in the journal *Musik-Texte*, no. 91 (November 2001: 69ff.)) be interpreted as a mere "slip up" (see in particular the report that appeared in *Libération* on September 19, 2001: "*Stockhausen dérape*" [Stockhausen slips up])? Stockhausen did indeed go back on his statements; he has constantly disavowed their substance. It nonetheless remains that his

transfiguration of this event that shook the world seems to me at least to need to be placed under the sign of an aestheticization of politics inherited from Wagner: "Spirits achieve with one act [i.e., September 11, 2001] something which we in music could never dream of," Stockhausen continued. "People practice ten years madly, fanatically, for a concert. And then die. . . . There are people who are so concentrated on this single performance, and then five thousand people are driven to Resurrection. In one moment." It is certainly no "accident" if this unity of bodies in redemption, if this being-a-musical-body as being-bound [*liaison*] in the supreme unbinding [*déliaison*] so resembles the "we will be one" stated by Wagner in *The Artwork of the Future*. The seven-day operatic project of *Licht* (which presents itself as an ultra-*Tetralogy*); the construction of architectural spaces that, at least since the famous sphere designed for the 1970 Osaka Universal Exposition, are situated in the lineage of Bayreuth—all of these signs, with their insistence on the lexicon of communitarian "redemption" through and in music, draw Stockhausen's positions closer to the *form* of Wagnerian political motifs, if not to their content. (Stockhausen's biography during the Second World War should certainly prohibit us from projecting the same sinister content into his works, but what remains in question is his recurrent vision of the political as a work of art. On this point, I refer the reader to Philippe Lacoue-Labarthe and Jean-Luc Nancy, "The Nazi Myth," trans. Brian Holmes, *Critical Inquiry* 16 [Winter 1990]: 291–312, and particularly 303: "In founding Bayreuth, [Wagner's] aim will be deliberately political: it will be that of the unification of the German people, through celebration and theatrical ceremonial. . . . And it is no doubt in this fundamental sense that one must understand the exigency of a 'total work of art.' The totalization is not only aesthetic: it beckons to the political.")

6. George Maciunas, "Neo-Dada in Music, Theater, Poetry, Art," in *Fluxus: Selections from the Gilbert and Lila Silverman Collection*, ed. Clive Phillpot and Jon Hendricks (New York: Museum of Modern Art, 1988), 25–27.
7. On this point, see Eric Michaud, "De Fluxus à Beuys: La fascination du politique," in *L'oeuvre d'art totale* (Paris: Editions du Centre National de la recherche scientifique, 1995).

8. Project addressed in December 1958 to the organizer of the summer courses in Darmstadt (in Paik, *Du Cheval à Christo*).
9. Marin Mersenne, *Les Question théologiques, physiques, morales et mathématiques: Où chacun trouvera du contentement et de l'exercice* (Paris: Henry Geunon, 1634). (Translation mine.—Trans.)
10. Glenn Gould, "Of Time and Time Beaters," in *The Glenn Gould Reader*, ed. Tim Page (New York: Vintage Books, , 1984), 404.
11. See Denis Fortier, "Le boeuf sur la 'toile'" in *Le Monde*, January 21, 1996. The orchestra conductor can be "filmed by a video camera whose images are transmitted by satellite to the different studios at the same time as the sound." The journalist specifies that "Frank Sinatra's album *Duet* and Patricia Kaas's *Je te dis vous* were recorded this way." (Translations mine.—Trans.)
12. Gabriel Tarde, *The Laws of Imitation,* trans. Elsie C. Parsons (New York: Henry Holt, 1903; reprint, Charleston, S.C.: BiblioBazaar, 2009), 70.
13. Ibid., 77.
14. Ibid., 84.
15. Michel Foucault, in *Discipline and Punish* (trans. Alan Sheridan [New York: Vintage, 1995], 317n3) reports that Jeremy Bentham, the inventor of the panopticon, "had also imagined acoustic surveillance, operated by means of pipes leading from the cells to the central tower." "He abandoned the idea, perhaps because he could not introduce into it the principle of dissymmetry and prevent the prisoners from hearing the inspector as well as the inspector hearing them. Julius tried to develop a system of dissymmetrical listening."
16. Sigmund Freud, *New Introductory Lectures on Psycho-Analysis*, trans. James Strachey (New York: Norton Standard Edition, 1990), 55.
17. In the chapter of his *Introduction to the Sociology of Music* devoted to the orchestra conductor (Theodor Adorno, *Introduction to the Sociology of Music*, trans. E. B. Ashton [New York: Seabury Press, 1976], 106; translation modified—Trans.), Adorno does indeed refer to Freud's "Group Psychology and the Analysis of the Ego" (1921, trans. James Strachey; New York: Bartleby.com, 2010). Elsewhere, concerning fans of jazz, Adorno recalled, not without condescension, that they nicknamed themselves "jitterbugs," or nervous

insects (see "Perennial Fashion—Jazz," in *Prisms*, trans. Sherry Weber and Samuel Weber [Cambridge, Mass.: MIT Press, 1981], 119–32). What would he have said of this electrical conduction that grabs hold of bodies during rock concerts or rave parties, that takes them and makes them consist by crystallizing them into a mass? Without an orchestra conductor, and under the figure of the very opposition to orchestral discipline, these telesthesiac crystallizations are nonetheless the distant inheritance of the conducted public concert that appeared in the eighteenth century and was generalized in the nineteenth.

18. Freud, "Group Psychology," 5.
19. Here, I refer the reader to Philippe Lacoue-Labarthe and Jean-Luc Nancy's reading of this text by Freud: "La panique politique," in *Cahiers Confrontations*, no. 2 ("L'état cellulaire") (Paris: Aubier, 1979).
20. Roland Barthes, "Rasch," in *The Responsibility of Forms*, trans. Richard Howard (Berkeley: University of California Press, 1985), 299: "I hear what beats in the body, what beats the body, or better: I hear this body that beats."
21. György Ligeti, in the book accompanying the compact disk *Works for Piano: Etudes, Musica ricercata* (Sony, 1996).
22. Jonathan Cott, *Conversations with Glenn Gould* (Chicago: University of Chicago Press, 2005), 34.
23. I wasn't able to read Charles Rosen's remarkable work *The Romantic Generation* (Cambridge, Mass.: Harvard University Press, 1998) until the moment when this book was almost finished. One finds in it more than one consideration of Chopin's fingerings that support my arguments. After having analyzed many passages from the *Etudes* where the weak or marginal fingers find themselves in an almost "soloist" position, Rosen writes: "His use of fifth finger and thumb put Chopin in direct opposition to the reigning contemporary piano pedagogy, the ideal of which was to make all fingers equally powerful and nimble. Chopin insisted that each finger was fundamentally different in character, and that the performer should try to exploit that difference" (368).
24. Helmut Lachenmann, "Des paradis éphémères," first published in the program of the Festival d'automne in Paris, then reprinted in

German in Helmut Lachenann, *Musik als existentielle Erfahrung, Schriften 1966–1995* (Leipzig: Bretikopf & Härtel, 1996). (Translation mine.—Trans.)

25. Cited by Hans-Peter Jahn, "Salut für Helmut" in the booklet for the compact disk *Helmut Lachenmann, Solo Pieces* (Auvidis, 1995).
26. Brilliantly analyzed by Charles Rosen in *The Romantic Generation*: "Here, in the last pages of the 'Abegg' Variations, Schumann plays the motto theme A-B-E-G-G (B in German notation is the English B-flat) not by sounding the last four notes but by taking them away, one by one. . . .This is the first time in history that a melody is signified not by the attack but by the release of a series of notes" (10). Or again: "In *Carnaval* at the end of 'Paganini' . . . after playing the four resounding thirds with full pedal, the pianist depresses the keys of the next chord without allowing the hammers to strike, and then changes the pedal. . . . As the other sounds die away, there is an extraordinary auditory illusion: the notes of the chord appear with what seems like a crescendo. This is probably the first use of piano harmonics by themselves." (25). In *Ein Kinderspiel*, the piece titled *Filter-Schaukel* systematically exploits these techniques.
27. Helmut Lachenmann, *Musik mit Bildern* ("music with images") after texts by Hans Christian Andersen, Gudrun Ensslin, and Leonardo da Vinci, 1997.
28. This is why I would be very tempted to oppose, in this dwindling twentieth century, Stockhausen's operatic heptalogy and the singular work of Lachenmann as two polar figures of embodiment. In a recent interview about his *Little Match Girl*, Lachenmann declared, "[Stockhausen] at bottom is aiming for a total conception of music, that englobes all the senses in a magical way and wants to synthesize all levels of human perception" (See "Les sons représentent des événements naturels," in the program for *La Petite fille aux allumettes*, Festival d'Automne-Opéra National de Paris, September 2001).
29. Walter Benjamin, "Die glückliche Hand," in *Gesammelte Schriften*, vol. 4, part 2, ed. Tillman Rexroth (Frankfurt am Main: Suhrkamp Verlag, 1972), 776. (Translation mine.—Trans.)

P.S.

1. Franz Kafka, *Diaries, 1910–1923*, ed. Max Brod, translated from the German by Joseph Kresh (New York: Schocken Books, 1988), 9–10. This scene was set to music in a gripping way by György Kurtág in 1985 in his *Kafka-Fragmente,* op. 24, for soprano and violin (III, 12: *Szene in der Elektrischen*).